Betty Crocker's

RED SPOON COLLECTION™

BEST RECIPES FOR LOW-CALORIE MICROWAVING

PRENTICE HALL

New York London Toronto Sydney Tokyo Singapore

Prentice Hall
15 Columbus Circle
New York, New York 10023

Published simultaneously in Canada by Prentice Hall Canada Inc.

PRENTICE HALL and colophon are registered
trademarks of Simon & Schuster, Inc.

BETTY CROCKER is a registered trademark
of General Mills, Inc.

RED SPOON COLLECTION is a trademark of General Mills, Inc.

Library of Congress Cataloging-in-Publication Data

Best recipes for low-calorie microwaving.—1st ed.
    p. cm.—(Betty Crocker's Red Spoon collection)
  Includes index.
    1. Low-calorie diet—Recipes. 2. Microwave cookery. I. Series.
RM222.2.B458 1990
641.5′635—dc20   89-8399
                                            CIP

Manufactured in the United States of America

10 9 8 7 6 5 4 3 2 1

First Prentice Hall Edition

Front Cover: Chicken Cacciatore

CONTENTS

INTRODUCTION

Of all cooking techniques, microwave cooking is one of the greatest innovations for calorie watchers. Microwaves cook food rapidly with little or no added fat, a boon to good nutrition. When foods are cooked with the addition of a flavorful liquid and covered, the microwave oven acts like a steamer, making every calorie go just a little bit farther on flavor. Microwave ovens make for delicious quick cooking with a minimum of fuss. It is comforting to know that rich-tasting, lower-calorie dishes are mere minutes away—no waiting around for long-simmering stews and slow-cooking roasts, while your resolve to eat healthy crumbles with each tick of the clock.

To take full advantage of your microwave oven's potential for lean cooking, you'll want to understand how the microwave works.

How Microwaves Work

Microwaves are radiant energy, like radio and television waves. They do not travel long distances; their energy quickly fades, which is why microwaves cook small pieces of food better than they cook large pieces. Microwaves are deflected by metal, and it is dangerous to place metal utensils in the microwave oven. (For a listing of microwavable equipment, turn to page 97 in Red Spoon Tips.) Microwaves travel through glass, paper, most plastics and wood, and they are absorbed by food, which contains moisture.

Water, fat and sugar molecules in food attract microwaves like magnets. The microwaves cause the molecules to vibrate, resulting in friction that heats and cooks the food. Microwaves approach a food from all angles simultaneously. Because they penetrate only about 1 inch beyond the food surface, much of the cooking is done by conduction of heat, just the way conventional cooking works. Foods cooked conventionally continue to cook (by conduction) for a brief time after they have been removed from the heat source. The same is true of microwave-cooked foods. Some microwave-cooked foods are best removed from the microwave oven just before they have finished cooking, because they will continue to cook while standing.

Microwave ovens produce a finite number of microwaves. If one potato is placed in the oven, all of the energy will focus on that potato. Two potatoes will have to share the energy and will take longer to cook than one potato. Three potatoes will take longer than two, and so on.

Microwave Safety

Although glass, ceramic, wood, plastic and wicker containers by themselves don't absorb microwaves and get hot, the food cooked in them does, and hot food can make a dish uncomfortably (or dangerously) hot to the touch. It is best to use pot holders when removing dishes from the microwave oven.

When the oven door is opened, the microwaves automatically stop. The manufacture of microwave ovens is carefully regulated to prevent radiation leakage. Periodically check to see that the door is undamaged and the seal is tight. Microwave ovens can be safer than stove tops for children: no open flames or exposed coil burners. (As always, adult supervision is recommended for young or inexperienced cooks.)

Your Microwave Oven

Microwave ovens differ in wattage. The recipes in this book were tested using countertop microwave ovens with 625 to 700 watts. If you are using a less powerful oven, cooking times must be lengthened. Because power settings vary from one manufacturer to another, and because the power output of the oven can vary with current levels at different times of day, cooking times will vary. This is why we usually give a cooking time range. Always check for doneness at the minimum cooking time. Some microwave ovens have "hot spots" that cook faster than others. It is important to stir or rotate a dish whenever a recipe indicates to do so.

Our recipe testing was done with foods taken directly from their normal storage areas, whether the refrigerator (eggs, milk, meat or fish), freezer (frozen vegetables) or kitchen shelf (dry goods, canned foods). Use the power setting first given in the directions, and change only to a different setting when directed to do so. Some foods cook best when covered tightly; use a lid or microwave-safe plastic wrap with an edge or corner turned back. Loose covering prevents spattering; use waxed paper, microwavable paper toweling or a napkin.

To make the most of wonderful, fresh produce, turn to Microwaving Fresh Vegetables (page 99) for an at-a-glance reference. Cooking with the microwave oven is fast and, best of all, simple with our quality-tested recipes. We hope that you enjoy this collection of delicious, low-calorie main dishes, whether with family or friends.

· 1 ·

VEGETARIAN FARE

Scrambled Eggs with Melted Cheddar

2 tablespoons margarine or butter
8 eggs, slightly beaten
1 can (12 ounces) whole kernel corn with peppers, drained
1 cup shredded Cheddar cheese (about 4 ounces)
½ cup milk
½ teaspoon dried basil leaves
½ teaspoon salt
⅛ teaspoon pepper
6 tomato slices
Dill

Place margarine in 2-quart microwavable casserole. Microwave uncovered on high until melted, 30 to 45 seconds. Mix remaining ingredients except tomato slices and dill; pour into casserole. Microwave uncovered, stirring every 2 minutes, until eggs are set but still moist, 8 to 10 minutes. Garnish with tomato slices and dill. Serve with Canadian bacon and toasted English muffins, if desired.

Curried Scrambled Eggs

6 SERVINGS; 260 CALORIES PER SERVING

1 cup water
1 teaspoon margarine or butter
½ teaspoon salt
1 cup uncooked instant rice
1 medium green pepper, chopped (about 1 cup)
1 medium onion, chopped (about ½ cup)
1 to 1½ teaspoons curry powder
¼ cup margarine or butter
8 eggs, slightly beaten
½ cup milk
½ teaspoon salt
1 medium tomato, chopped (about ¾ cup)

Mix water, 1 teaspoon margarine, ½ teaspoon salt and the rice in 1-quart microwavable casserole. Cover tightly and microwave on high until rice is tender and water is absorbed, 4 to 6 minutes. Place green pepper, onion, curry powder and ¼ cup margarine in 2-quart microwavable casserole. Cover tightly and microwave on high until tender, 3 to 5 minutes; stir. Mix rice, eggs, milk and ½ teaspoon salt; pour over onion mixture. Cover tightly and microwave, stirring every 2 minutes, until eggs are thickened but still moist, 3½ to 5 minutes. Sprinkle with tomato. Serve with toasted raisin bread, if desired.

Home-style Scrambled Eggs

4 SERVINGS; 130 CALORIES PER SERVING

4 eggs
3 tablespoons water
¾ teaspoon salt
1 cup cubed cooked potato (1 medium)
3 tablespoons finely chopped onion
1 small zucchini, halved and sliced
1 tomato, chopped

Beat eggs, water and salt with fork in 1½-quart microwavable casserole. Stir in potato, onion and zucchini. Cover tightly and microwave on high, stirring every minute, until eggs are puffy and set but still moist, 4 to 5 minutes. (Eggs will continue to cook while standing.) Stir in tomato.

Creamy Eggs with Blue Cheese

4 SERVINGS; 230 CALORIES PER SERVING

*1 medium onion, chopped (about
  ½ cup)*
2 tablespoons margarine or butter
8 eggs, slightly beaten
½ cup milk
2 tablespoons finely crumbled blue cheese
½ teaspoon salt
⅛ teaspoon pepper

Place onion and margarine in 2-quart microwavable casserole. Microwave uncovered on high until onion is tender, 3 to 4 minutes. Mix eggs, milk, cheese, salt and pepper; pour into casserole. Microwave uncovered, stirring every 2 minutes, until eggs are set but still moist, 6 to 8 minutes. (Eggs will continue to cook while standing.)

Chinese-style Casserole

4 SERVINGS; 190 CALORIES PER SERVING

Oriental Sauce (below)
*1 can (16 ounces) bean sprouts, rinsed
  and drained*
*1 can (8 ounces) sliced water chestnuts,
  drained*
*½ cup chopped green pepper (about
  1 small)*
¼ cup chopped onion (about 1 small)
6 eggs, beaten
1 tablespoon chopped pimiento
¾ teaspoon salt

Prepare Oriental Sauce. Mix bean sprouts, water chestnuts, green pepper and onion in 1½-quart casserole. Cover tightly and microwave on high 3 minutes; stir. Cover and microwave until vegetables are hot, 2 to 3 minutes longer; drain.

Stir in eggs, pimiento and salt. Cover tightly and microwave on high 2 minutes; stir. Cover and microwave until eggs are set but still moist, 1½ to 4 minutes longer. Spoon Oriental Sauce over each serving.

ORIENTAL SAUCE

⅔ cup water
3 tablespoons soy sauce
1 tablespoon cornstarch
1 teaspoon sugar
1 teaspoon vinegar

Mix all ingredients in 2-cup measure. Microwave uncovered on high, stirring every minute, until mixture boils and thickens, 3 to 4 minutes.

Following pages: Curried Scrambled Eggs

Three-Cheese Pie

8 SERVINGS; 230 CALORIES PER SERVING

1 cup shredded Cheddar cheese (about
   4 ounces)
1 cup shredded mozzarella cheese (about
   4 ounces)
1 cup shredded Monterey Jack cheese
   (about 4 ounces)
1 medium onion, chopped
2 tablespoons all-purpose flour
4 eggs
1 cup milk
1/2 teaspoon salt
1/2 teaspoon dry mustard
1/2 teaspoon Worcestershire sauce
2 medium tomatoes, sliced

Mix cheeses, onion and flour. Spread in greased microwavable pie plate, 10 × 1½ inches, or microwavable quiche dish, 9 × 1½ inches. Beat eggs slightly; beat in milk, salt, mustard and Worcestershire sauce. Pour over cheese mixture. Elevate pie plate on inverted microwavable plate in microwave. Microwave uncovered on medium-high (70%) 8 minutes; rotate pie plate ½ turn. Microwave until center is set, 7 to 10 minutes longer. Let stand 5 minutes. Arrange tomato slices around edge of pie, overlapping slices slightly.

Eggs and Broccoli

6 SERVINGS; 300 CALORIES PER SERVING

1 package (10 ounces) frozen chopped
   broccoli
1/2 teaspoon salt
12 hard-cooked eggs, cut lengthwise into
   fourths
1 can (11 ounces) condensed Cheddar
   cheese soup
3/4 cup milk
1 jar (2 ounces) diced pimiento, drained
1 tablespoon snipped fresh parsley or
   1 teaspoon parsley flakes
1/2 teaspoon dry mustard
3/4 teaspoon snipped fresh basil leaves or
   1/4 teaspoon dried basil leaves
1/8 teaspoon onion powder
3 drops red pepper sauce
1 cup crushed corn chips or potato chips

Rinse broccoli in cold water to separate; drain. Spread broccoli in rectangular microwavable dish, 12 × 7½ × 2 inches or 10 × 6 × 1½ inches; sprinkle with salt. Arrange eggs cut sides up on broccoli. Mix remaining ingredients except corn chips in 4-cup microwavable measure, stirring until smooth. Microwave uncovered on high stirring after 2 minutes, until hot and bubbly, 3½ to 5 minutes. Pour over eggs. Cover tightly and microwave 4 minutes. Sprinkle with chips and rotate dish ½ turn. Microwave until hot and bubbly, 2½ to 4½ minutes longer.

Bean and Cheese Turnovers

Red Salsa (below)
1 can (8 ounces) kidney beans, drained
(reserve liquid)
1 clove garlic, finely chopped
4 flour tortillas (8-inch)
1 cup part skim ricotta cheese (8 ounces)
¼ cup grated Parmesan cheese
¼ cup chopped green onions (with tops)
1 tablespoon snipped fresh cilantro or
*   1 teaspoon dried cilantro leaves*

Prepare Red Salsa. Mash beans and garlic. (Add 1 to 2 tablespoons reserved bean liquid if beans are dry.) Place tortillas on ungreased cookie sheet. Spread about ¼ cup of the bean mixture on half of each tortilla to within ½ inch of edge. Mix cheeses, onions and cilantro; spread over beans. Fold tortillas over filling. Place double layer of microwavable paper towels in rectangular microwavable dish, 12 × 7½ × 2 inches. Place turnovers with folds to outside edges in dish. Cover with waxed paper and microwave on high 2 minutes; rotate ½ turn. Microwave until hot, 2 to 5 minutes longer. Serve with Red Salsa.

RED SALSA

1 large clove garlic, finely chopped
1 cup chopped tomato
¼ cup chopped green onions (with tops)
2 to 3 teaspoons chopped jalapeño pepper (about ½ small)
1½ teaspoons finely snipped fresh cilantro, if desired
1½ teaspoons lemon juice
1 teaspoon snipped fresh oregano leaves or ½ teaspoon dried oregano leaves

Mix all ingredients; cover and refrigerate at least 1 hour.

Southwestern Bean Soup with Chilies

1 medium onion, sliced
1 large clove garlic, crushed
2 tablespoons margarine or butter
1 can (28 ounces) whole tomatoes, undrained
1 can (20 ounces) kidney beans, drained
1 can (16 ounces) pinto beans, drained
1 can (4 ounces) chopped green chilies, drained
1 tablespoon chili powder
1/4 teaspoon ground coriander
1/2 cup shredded Cheddar cheese (2 ounces)
1/2 cup shredded Monterey Jack cheese (2 ounces)

Place onion, garlic and margarine in 3-quart microwavable casserole. Cover tightly and microwave on high until onion is tender, 2 to 4 minutes. Stir in remaining ingredients except cheeses; break up tomatoes. Cover tightly and microwave 10 minutes; stir.

Cover tightly and microwave until hot and bubbly, 6 to 9 minutes longer. Stir in Cheddar cheese and 1/2 cup of the Monterey Jack cheese. Cover tightly and let stand until cheese is melted, about 5 minutes. Sprinkle each serving with remaining Monterey Jack cheese.

Red Kidney Bean Soup

1 can (16 ounces) red kidney beans, drained (reserve liquid)
1 cup chopped onion (about 1 large)
1 cup chopped celery (about 2 medium stalks)
2 cloves garlic, finely chopped
1 tablespoon reduced-calorie margarine
2 cups chicken broth
1/2 teaspoon salt
1 teaspoon ground cumin
1 teaspoon chili powder
1/4 teaspoon ground thyme
1 tablespoon lemon juice

Place 1/2 of the beans and reserved liquid in blender container. Cover and blend on high speed until almost smooth, about 1 minute. Microwave onion, celery and garlic in margarine in 2-quart microwavable casserole uncovered on high 2 minutes; stir. Microwave until onion is tender, 1 to 2 minutes longer. Stir in remaining ingredients except lemon juice. Cover tightly and microwave 5 minutes; stir. Cover and microwave until hot and bubbly, 5 to 7 minutes longer. Stir in lemon juice.

Spicy Beans with Squash

4 SERVINGS; 100 CALORIES PER SERVING

1½ cups ¼-inch slices yellow squash
(about 1½ medium)
1½ cups ¼-inch slices zucchini (about
1½ medium)
1 cup cubed Hubbard or acorn squash
(about 4 ounces)
½ cup chopped onion (about 1 medium)
½ cup chicken broth
1 to 2 tablespoons chopped jalapeño
pepper (about 1 small)
1 large clove garlic, finely chopped
2 cans (16 ounces) kidney beans, drained
¼ cup snipped fresh cilantro

Place all ingredients except beans and cilantro in 2-quart microwavable casserole. Cover tightly and microwave on high 6 minutes; stir in beans. Cover tightly and microwave until vegetables are tender, 4 to 6 minutes longer. Stir in cilantro.

Herbed Vegetables with Lentils

4 SERVINGS; 75 CALORIES PER SERVING

2 cups chicken broth
¾ cup dried lentils (about 4 ounces)
1 cup sliced zucchini (about 1 small)
1 cup sliced yellow squash (about 1 small)
½ cup sliced green onions (with tops)
1½ teaspoons snipped fresh oregano
leaves or ½ teaspoon dried oregano
leaves
¼ teaspoon ground thyme
2 large cloves garlic, finely chopped
1 jar (2 ounces) diced pimientos, drained
2 tablespoons grated Parmesan cheese

Place chicken broth with lentils in 2-quart microwavable casserole. Cover tightly and microwave on high 20 minutes. Stir in zucchini, squash, onions, oregano, thyme and garlic. Cover and microwave on medium (50%) 5 minutes; stir in pimientos. Microwave uncovered until vegetables are crisp-tender and mixture is of desired consistency, 2 to 4 minutes longer. Sprinkle with cheese.

Following pages: Spicy Beans with Squash

Garbanzo Beans with Spinach

4 SERVINGS; 160 CALORIES PER SERVING

1 can (16 ounces) garbanzo beans,
   drained (reserve liquid)
1 package (10 ounces) frozen chopped
   spinach
1 clove garlic, finely chopped
1/4 teaspoon salt
1/8 teaspoon pepper
1/8 to 1/4 teaspoon ground nutmeg

Place 1 tablespoon reserved bean liquid and remaining ingredients except beans in 1½-quart microwavable casserole. Cover tightly and microwave on high 7 minutes; stir in beans. Microwave uncovered until moisture evaporates, 2 to 5 minutes longer.

Vegetarian Spaghetti

6 SERVINGS; 270 CALORIES PER SERVING

4 cups 1/4-inch slices zucchini (about
   1 pound)
1 can (28 ounces) whole tomatoes
1 can (12 ounces) tomato paste
1 can (4 ounces) mushroom stems and
   pieces, drained
1/2 cup dry red wine
1/2 cup finely chopped onion (about
   1 medium)
1 clove garlic, finely chopped
1 tablespoon snipped fresh parsley or
   2 teaspoons dried parsley flakes
1 tablespoon snipped fresh oregano leaves
   or 2 teaspoons dried oregano leaves
2 teaspoons sugar
1 teaspoon salt
4 cups hot cooked spaghetti
1 cup shredded mozzarella cheese (about
   4 ounces)
1/3 cup grated Parmesan cheese

Mix zucchini and tomatoes (with liquid). Break up tomatoes with fork. Stir in remaining ingredients except spaghetti and cheese in 3-quart microwavable casserole. Cover tightly and microwave on high 8 minutes; stir. Cover and microwave until zucchini is tender and mixture is bubbly, 8 to 12 minutes longer. Serve sauce over hot spaghetti; sprinkle with cheeses.

· 2 ·

CHICKEN AND TURKEY

Ginger Chicken with Vegetables   7 SERVINGS; 230 CALORIES PER SERVING

2½- to 3-pound whole broiler-fryer
  chicken
2 tablespoons margarine or butter, melted
¼ teaspoon paprika
¼ teaspoon ground ginger
2 packages (6 ounces each) frozen pea
  pods
1 medium onion, chopped (about ½ cup)
½ teaspoon ground turmeric
¼ teaspoon ground ginger
2 tablespoons margarine or butter
8 ounces medium mushrooms
1 teaspoon salt
2 teaspoons lemon juice
8 cherry tomatoes, cut into halves

Fold wings of chicken across back with tips touching. Tie drumsticks to tail. Place chicken breast side down in square microwavable dish, 8 × 8 × 2 inches. Microwave uncovered on high 12 minutes. Turn chicken breast side up. Mix 2 tablespoons margarine, the paprika, and ¼ teaspoon ginger; brush over chicken. Microwave uncovered until juices run clear when thigh is pricked, 10 to 14 minutes. Cover and keep warm.

Rinse pea pods under running cold water to separate; drain. Combine onion, turmeric, ¼ teaspoon ginger and 2 tablespoons margarine in 1½-quart microwavable casserole. Cover tightly and microwave until onion is tender, 2 to 4 minutes; add pea pods, mushrooms, salt and lemon juice. Cover tightly and microwave until pea pods are tender, 4 to 7 minutes. Stir in tomatoes; let stand 3 minutes. Serve vegetables with chicken.

Herbed Chicken

2½- to 3-pound broiler-fryer chicken
2 tablespoons margarine or butter
2 tablespoons olive or vegetable oil
¼ cup finely chopped onion
¼ cup lemon juice
2 tablespoons Worcestershire sauce
1½ teaspoons snipped fresh basil leaves
    or ½ teaspoon dried basil leaves
¾ teaspoon snipped fresh marjoram
    leaves or ¼ teaspoon dried marjoram
    leaves
¾ teaspoon snipped fresh oregano leaves
    or ¼ teaspoon dried oregano leaves
2 large cloves garlic, finely chopped

Cut chicken into pieces; cut each breast half into halves and remove skin. Place margarine and oil in rectangular microwavable dish, 12 × 7½ × 2 inches. Microwave uncovered on high until margarine is melted, 45 to 60 seconds. Stir in remaining ingredients except chicken. Place chicken in dish, turning to coat with herb mixture. Arrange with thickest parts to outside edges in dish. Cover with waxed paper and microwave on high 10 minutes; rotate dish ½ turn. Microwave until thickest pieces are done, 6 to 10 minutes longer.

Chicken with Apricots

2½- to 3-pound broiler-fryer chicken
2 tablespoons soy sauce
2 tablespoons honey
1 tablespoon vegetable oil
1 tablespoon chili sauce
½ teaspoon ground ginger
⅛ teaspoon cayenne pepper
1 can (16 ounces) apricot halves in juice,
    drained

Cut chicken into pieces; cut each breast half into halves and remove skin. Arrange chicken with thickest parts to outside edges in microwavable dish, 12 × 7½ × 2 inches. Mix remaining ingredients except apricots; brush over chicken, turning pieces to coat. Cover tightly and microwave on high 10 minutes. Brush with the liquid mixture; rotate dish ½ turn. Cover and microwave until thickest pieces are done, 6 to 10 minutes longer. Arrange apricots around chicken; brush chicken and apricots with the liquid. Microwave uncovered until apricots are hot, about 1 minute.

Chicken with Artichokes and Grapes
7 SERVINGS; 230 CALORIES PER SERVING

2½- to 3-pound broiler-fryer chicken
6 slices bacon, cut up
½ teaspoon salt
½ teaspoon paprika
1½ teaspoons snipped fresh tarragon
  leaves or ½ teaspoon dried tarragon leaves
4 ounces mushrooms, sliced (about 1½
  cups) or 1 can (4 ounces) mushroom
  stems and pieces, drained
½ cup dry white wine or apple juice
1 tablespoon cornstarch
2 tablespoons cold water
1 can (14 ounces) artichoke hearts,
  drained and cut into halves
2 cups seedless green or red grapes

Cut chicken into pieces; cut each breast half into halves and remove skin. Place bacon in microwavable dish, 12 × 7½ × 2 inches. Cover loosely and microwave on high until crisp, 6 to 9 minutes. Remove with slotted spoon and drain; reserve. Drain bacon fat from dish. Arrange chicken pieces with thickest parts to outside edges in dish. Mix salt, paprika and tarragon; sprinkle over chicken. Place mushrooms on chicken. Pour wine over chicken and mushrooms. Cover tightly and microwave on high 10 minutes; rotate dish ½ turn. Microwave until thickest pieces are done, 6 to 10 minutes. Remove chicken; keep warm.

Mix cornstarch and cold water; stir into liquid in dish. Microwave uncovered, stirring every minute, until slightly thickened, 3 to 4 minutes. Stir in artichokes and grapes. Microwave uncovered 2 minutes. Pour over chicken; sprinkle with bacon.

Creole Chicken
6 SERVINGS; 220 CALORIES PER SERVING

2½- to 3-pound broiler-fryer chicken,
  cut up
2 medium onions, chopped
1 clove garlic, chopped
1 green pepper, chopped
1 can (16 ounces) stewed tomatoes
1 can (8 ounces) tomato sauce
1 teaspoon salt
½ teaspoon ground thyme
½ teaspoon red pepper sauce
¼ teaspoon cayenne red pepper
1½ cups sliced okra

Arrange chicken with thickest pieces to outside edge in 3-quart microwavable casserole. Cover tightly and microwave on high 15 minutes; drain. Mix remaining ingredients. Pour evenly over chicken. Cover tightly and microwave until thickest pieces of chicken are done and okra is tender, 10 to 14 minutes.

Following pages: Creole Chicken

Mexican Chicken with Rice

6 SERVINGS; 230 CALORIES PER SERVING

2½- to 3-pound broiler-fryer chicken,
    cut up
¾ teaspoon salt
¼ to ½ teaspoon paprika
¼ teaspoon pepper
1½ cups hot water
1½ teaspoons instant chicken bouillon
½ cup uncooked instant rice
1 medium onion, chopped (about ½ cup)
1 teaspoon garlic salt
1½ teaspoons snipped fresh oregano leaves
    or ½ teaspoon dried oregano leaves
⅛ teaspoon ground turmeric
1 bay leaf
1 package (10 ounces) frozen green peas,
    thawed and drained

Arrange chicken with thickest parts to outside edge in 3-quart microwavable casserole. Sprinkle with salt, paprika and pepper. Cover tightly and microwave on high 14 minutes. Remove chicken and drain fat from casserole. Mix hot water, instant bouillon (dry), instant rice, onion, garlic salt, oregano, turmeric, bay leaf and peas in casserole; top with chicken. Cover tightly and microwave on high until rice is tender and meat is no longer pink, 10 to 14 minutes. Let stand covered 5 minutes. Remove bay leaf. Garnish with pimiento strips and pitted ripe olives, if desired.

Lemon Chicken

6 SERVINGS; 190 CALORIES PER SERVING

2½- to 3-pound broiler-fryer chicken,
    cut up
½ cup dry white wine
¼ cup lemon juice
2 tablespoons vegetable oil
1 teaspoon paprika
1 lemon, thinly sliced
1 clove garlic, crushed
1 lemon, thinly sliced
Paprika

Place chicken in 2-quart microwavable casserole. Mix wine, lemon juice, oil, 1 teaspoon paprika, 1 lemon and garlic; pour over chicken pieces. Cover and refrigerate at least 3 hours.

Remove chicken and lemon slices from marinade. Discard lemon slices; reserve marinade. Arrange chicken with thickest parts to outside edge in casserole. Cover tightly and microwave on high 12 minutes. Place chicken bone sides down on grill, 5 to 6 inches from medium coals. Cover and grill, turning and brushing 2 or 3 times with reserved marinade, until chicken is done, 15 to 20 minutes. Roll edges of fresh lemon slices in paprika; arrange around chicken. Garnish with celery leaves, if desired.

Tarragon Chicken

6 SERVINGS; 270 CALORIES PER SERVING

1 cup chicken broth or bouillon
3 medium carrots, sliced
1 tablespoon snipped fresh tarragon
leaves or 1 teaspoon dried tarragon
leaves
1½ teaspoons salt
⅛ teaspoon pepper
1 bay leaf
2½- to 3-pound broiler-fryer chicken,
cut up
4 ounces mushrooms, sliced
2 stalks celery, sliced
1 medium onion, sliced
½ cup dry white wine
½ cup half-and-half
3 tablespoons all-purpose flour
1 egg yolk

Place broth, carrots, tarragon, salt, pepper and bay leaf in 3-quart microwavable casserole. Cover tightly and microwave on high until boiling, 5 to 8 minutes. Add chicken; spoon broth over top. Cover tightly and microwave 10 minutes; rotate casserole ½ turn. Add mushrooms, celery and onion. Cover tightly and microwave until thickest pieces of chicken are done, 8 to 13 minutes longer. Remove bay leaf. Remove chicken and vegetables to warm platter; keep warm.

Drain liquid from casserole; strain and reserve 1 cup. Pour reserved liquid and the wine into casserole. Mix half-and-half, flour and egg yolk until smooth; stir into wine mixture. Microwave uncovered on high stirring every minute, until thickened, 3 to 4 minutes. Serve with chicken. Garnish with fresh tarragon or parsley, if desired.

Barbecued Chicken

7 SERVINGS; 175 CALORIES PER SERVING

2½- to 3-pound broiler-fryer chicken,
cut up
¾ cup chili sauce
2 tablespoons honey
2 tablespoons soy sauce
1 teaspoon dry mustard
½ teaspoon prepared horseradish
½ teaspoon red pepper sauce

Arrange chicken, skin sides up with thickest parts to outside edges, in rectangular microwavable dish, 12 × 7½ × 2 inches. Mix remaining ingredients; pour over chicken. Cover with waxed paper and microwave on high 10 minutes. Spoon sauce over chicken; rotate dish ½ turn. Cover with waxed paper and microwave until thickest pieces are done, 6 to 10 minutes longer.

Plum-barbecued Chicken

6 SERVINGS; 150 CALORIES PER SERVING

3-pound broiler-fryer chicken, cut up
  and skinned
1 can (16 ounces) purple plums in juice,
  drained and pitted
1/4 cup chopped onion (about 1 small)
1/4 cup chili sauce
2 tablespoons lemon juice
1 tablespoon prepared mustard

Arrange chicken, meaty sides up with thickest parts to outside edges, in rectangular microwavable dish, 12 × 7½ × 2 inches. Place remaining ingredients in blender container. Cover and blend on medium speed until well blended. Pour over chicken. Cover with waxed paper and microwave on high 10 minutes. Place remaining ingredients in blender container. Cover and blend on medium speed until well blended. Spoon sauce over chicken; rotate dish ½ turn. Cover and microwave until thickest pieces are done, 6 to 10 minutes longer. Stir juices; spoon over chicken.

Chicken with Cauliflower and Peas

6 SERVINGS; 220 CALORIES PER SERVING

3-pound broiler-fryer chicken, cut up
  (about 8 pieces)
1 teaspoon salt
1 clove garlic, finely chopped
1½ teaspoons snipped fresh basil leaves
  or ½ teaspoon dried basil leaves
1/4 teaspoon paprika
1 medium onion, cut into 8 wedges
3 cups 1-inch cauliflower flowerets (about
  1 pound)
1 package (10 ounces) frozen green peas
1/2 teaspoon salt
1/8 teaspoon pepper

Cut each chicken breast half into halves. Arrange pieces, skin sides up with thickest parts to outside edge, in microwavable baking dish, 12 × 7½ × 2 inches. Sprinkle with 1 teaspoon salt, the garlic, basil and paprika. Add onion. Cover tightly and microwave on high 10 minutes.

Add cauliflower and peas; sprinkle with ½ teaspoon salt and the pepper. Rotate baking dish ½ turn. Cover tightly and microwave on high until thickest parts of chicken are done and vegetables are tender, 10 to 15 minutes. Uncover and let stand 3 minutes.

Chutney Chicken

3-pound broiler-fryer chicken, cut up
  and skinned
1/4 cup chopped chutney
1/4 cup lime juice
2 tablespoons finely chopped onion
2 tablespoons nonfat plain yogurt
1/2 teaspoon curry powder
1/4 teaspoon dry mustard
1 lime, cut into wedges

Remove excess fat from chicken. Mix all ingredients except chicken and lime in glass or plastic bowl or heavy plastic bag. Add chicken, turning to coat. Cover and refrigerate at least 2 hours.

Arrange chicken, meaty sides up with thickest parts to outside edges, in rectangular microwavable dish, $12 \times 7\frac{1}{2} \times 2$ inches. Pour marinade over chicken. Cover with waxed paper and microwave on high 10 minutes; spoon sauce over chicken. Rotate dish 1/2 turn. Microwave until thickest pieces are done, 6 to 10 minutes longer. Serve with lime wedges.

Chicken Cacciatore

2 1/2- to 3-pound broiler-fryer chicken,
  cut up
1 cup sliced mushrooms (about 3 ounces)
1 medium onion, chopped (about 1/2 cup)
1/4 cup sliced ripe olives
1/2 teaspoon salt
1 tablespoon snipped fresh oregano leaves
  or 1 teaspoon dried oregano leaves,
  crushed
1/4 teaspoon pepper
1 can (16 ounces) whole tomatoes,
  undrained
1 can (8 ounces) tomato sauce
2 cloves garlic, crushed
1 bay leaf
Snipped parsley
Hot cooked spaghetti

Arrange chicken, skin sides up with thickest parts to outside edge, in 3-quart microwavable casserole. Cover tightly and microwave on high 12 minutes; drain. Mix remaining ingredients except parsley and spaghetti; break up tomatoes with fork. Pour over chicken. Cover tightly and microwave 10 minutes; rearrange chicken. Cover tightly and microwave until thickest pieces of chicken are done, 7 to 12 minutes longer. Remove bay leaf. Sprinkle with parsley; serve with spaghetti.

Quick Chicken Kiev

6 SERVINGS; 265 CALORIES PER SERVING

1/4 cup margarine or butter, softened
1 tablespoon snipped chives or parsley
1/8 teaspoon garlic powder
6 small chicken breast halves (about
  3 pounds)
3 cups cornflakes, crushed (about
  1 1/2 cups)
2 tablespoons snipped parsley
1/2 teaspoon paprika
1/4 cup buttermilk or milk

Mix margarine, chives and garlic powder; shape into rectangle, 3 × 2 inches. Cover and freeze until firm, about 30 minutes.

Remove bones and skin from chicken breasts. Flatten each chicken breast to 1/4-inch thickness between plastic wrap. Cut margarine mixture crosswise into 6 pieces. Place 1 piece on center of each chicken breast. Fold long sides over margarine; fold ends up and secure with wooden pick. Mix cornflakes, parsley and paprika. Dip chicken into buttermilk; coat evenly with cornflake mixture.

Arrange coated chicken breast halves, seam sides down, on a microwavable rack in microwavable dish. Microwave uncovered on high 4 minutes; rotate dish 1/2 turn. Microwave uncovered until chicken is done, 4 to 6 minutes longer. Let stand uncovered 5 minutes.

Lemon-Dill Chicken

6 SERVINGS; 175 CALORIES PER SERVING

6 small chicken breast halves (about
  2 pounds)
2 tablespoons margarine or butter
1/4 cup dry white wine
1 tablespoon lemon juice
1/4 teaspoon salt
1/4 teaspoon snipped fresh dill or
  1/8 teaspoon dried dill weed
1/2 lemon, thinly sliced
2 tablespoons sliced green onions (with
  tops)

Remove skin and bones from chicken breasts. Place margarine in 3-quart microwavable casserole. Microwave uncovered on high until melted, about 1 1/2 minutes. Arrange chicken in margarine with thickest pieces to outside edge. Cover tightly and microwave on high 4 minutes. Mix wine, lemon juice, salt and dill weed; pour over chicken. Place lemon slices on chicken; rotate casserole 1/2 turn. Cover and microwave until chicken is done, 4 to 6 minutes longer. Let stand 5 minutes; sprinkle with onions.

Waldorf Chicken

6 SERVINGS; 240 CALORIES PER SERVING

6 small chicken breast halves (about
3 pounds), boned and skinned
3/4 cup unsweetened apple juice
1 tablespoon lemon juice
1/4 teaspoon salt
1/4 teaspoon ground ginger
1 tablespoon cornstarch
2 cups coarsely chopped unpared red
apples (about 2 medium)
1 cup diagonal slices celery (about
2 medium stalks)
3 tablespoons raisins
1 tablespoon sliced green onion (with top)

Place chicken, 1/2 cup of the apple juice, the lemon juice, salt and ginger in 3-quart microwavable casserole. Cover tightly and microwave on high 6 minutes; rotate 1/2 turn. Microwave until chicken is done, 6 to 8 minutes longer. Remove chicken; keep warm.

Mix remaining apple juice and the cornstarch; add to hot liquid. Microwave uncovered, stirring every minute until thickened, 3 to 4 minutes. Stir in remaining ingredients and microwave until hot, 2 to 3 minutes. For each serving, diagonally slice chicken breast, overlapping slices. Top with sauce.

Curried Cornish Hens with Apples

4 SERVINGS; 250 CALORIES PER SERVING

2 Rock Cornish hens (about 1 pound
each), split lengthwise
1/4 cup sherry
1/4 cup unsweetened apple juice
2 tablespoons soy sauce
1/2 to 1 teaspoon curry powder
1/4 teaspoon dry mustard
2 cloves garlic, crushed
2 cups thinly sliced unpared apples (about
2 medium)

Place hens, skin sides down, in rectangular microwavable baking dish, 12 × 7 1/2 × 2 inches, or heavy plastic bag. Mix remaining ingredients except apples; pour marinade over hens. Cover and refrigerate, turning hens occasionally, at least 6 hours.

Remove hens from marinade. Arrange apples in marinade in baking dish; place hens, skin sides up, on apples. Cover with waxed paper and microwave on high 10 minutes; spoon juices over top. Sprinkle with paprika. Cover and microwave until hens are done, 6 to 10 minutes longer.

Following pages: Lemon-Dill Chicken

Chicken–Wild Rice Casserole

6 SERVINGS; 280 CALORIES PER SERVING

Wild and White Rice (below)
¼ cup margarine or butter
⅓ cup all-purpose flour
1 teaspoon salt
⅛ teaspoon pepper
½ cup milk
1 cup chicken broth
2 cups cut-up cooked chicken
⅓ cup chopped green pepper
2 tablespoons slivered almonds
2 tablespoons chopped pimiento
1 can (4 ounces) mushroom stems and
* pieces, drained*

Prepare Wild and White Rice conventionally. Place margarine in 2-quart microwavable casserole. Microwave uncovered on high until melted, about 45 seconds. Stir in flour, salt and pepper. Stir milk and broth into flour mixture. Microwave, stirring every minute, until thickened, 4 to 5 minutes. Stir in rice and remaining ingredients. Cover and microwave until hot and bubbly, 5 to 8 minutes longer.

WILD AND WHITE RICE

¼ cup uncooked wild rice
⅔ cup water
½ teaspoon salt
¼ cup uncooked regular rice
½ cup water

Heat wild rice, ⅔ cup water and the salt to boiling in 1-quart saucepan; reduce heat. Cover and simmer 30 minutes. Add regular rice and ½ cup water. Heat to boiling; reduce heat. Cover and simmer 15 minutes. Remove from heat. Fluff rice with fork; cover and let stand 5 minutes.

Chicken Enchiladas

6 SERVINGS; 300 CALORIES PER SERVING

*1 medium onion, chopped (about
    ½ cup)*
2 cloves garlic, chopped
2 tablespoons vegetable oil
1½ cups chicken broth
1 to 2 tablespoons chili powder
*1 tablespoon snipped fresh oregano leaves
    or 1 teaspoon dried oregano leaves*
1 teaspoon ground cumin
1 teaspoon salt
1 can (8 ounces) tomato sauce
12 corn tortillas (6-inch)
3 cups shredded cooked chicken*
*½ cup shredded Monterey Jack or sharp
    Cheddar cheese (about 2 ounces)*

Place onion, garlic and oil in 2-quart microwavable casserole. Cover tightly and microwave on high until onion is tender, 2 to 3 minutes. Stir in broth, seasonings and tomato sauce. Cover tightly and microwave until hot and bubbly, 5 to 7 minutes. Dip tortillas into sauce to coat both sides. Spoon ¼ cup of the chicken onto each tortilla; roll tortilla around chicken.

Place 6 enchiladas, seam sides down, in square microwavable dish, 8 × 8 × 2 inches, or rectangular microwavable dish, 10 × 6 × 1½ inches. Pour half of the sauce over top. Repeat with remaining tortillas in a second microwavable dish. Pour remaining sauce over enchiladas. Cover tightly and microwave each dish separately on high until hot, 4 to 6 minutes. Sprinkle with cheese and serve with shredded lettuce, if desired.

*Use 2 forks to shred warm cooked chicken.

Chicken Spaghetti

1/2 cup water
1 large onion, chopped (about 1 cup)
1 teaspoon salt
1 teaspoon sugar
1 tablespoon snipped fresh oregano leaves
   or 1 teaspoon dried oregano leaves
2 teaspoons snipped fresh basil leaves or
   3/4 teaspoon dried basil leaves
3/4 teaspoon snipped fresh marjoram
   leaves or 1/4 teaspoon dried marjoram
   leaves
3/4 teaspoon snipped fresh rosemary leaves
   or 1/4 teaspoon dried rosemary leaves
1 clove garlic, crushed
1 bay leaf
1 can (8 ounces) tomato sauce
1 can (6 ounces) tomato paste
1/4 cup water
1 1/2 cups cut-up cooked chicken
6 cups hot cooked spaghetti

Mix 1/2 cup water and the chopped onion in 2-quart microwavable casserole. Cover tightly and microwave on high until onion is barely tender, 3 to 4 1/2 minutes. Stir in seasonings, tomato sauce, tomato paste and 1/4 cup water. Cover and microwave on high 5 minutes; stir in chicken. Microwave tightly covered on medium-low (30%) until hot, 15 to 18 minutes. Remove bay leaf. Serve sauce over spaghetti. Sprinkle with grated Parmesan cheese, if desired.

Oriental Turkey and Vegetables

1 package (16 ounces) frozen Oriental-
   style vegetables
1 can (10 3/4 ounces) condensed chicken
   broth
1 teaspoon finely chopped gingerroot
2 cups cut-up cooked turkey or chicken
3 tablespoons cornstarch
1/2 cup cold water
2 1/2 cups chow mein noodles

Place vegetables in 3-quart microwavable casserole. Cover tightly and microwave on high until almost tender, as directed in microwave directions on package. Stir in broth, gingerroot and turkey.

Mix cornstarch and water. Stir into vegetable mixture. Cover tightly and microwave 3 minutes; stir. Cover tightly and microwave, stirring every minute, until mixture thickens and boils, 5 to 6 minutes longer. Serve over chow mein noodles and, if desired, with soy sauce.

Turkey with Chipotle Sauce

4 SERVINGS; 195 CALORIES PER SERVING

Chipotle Sauce (below)
1 pound boneless turkey breast slices, cut-
  lets or turkey tenderloin steaks (^{1}/$_4$ to
  ^{1}/$_2$ inch thick)
^{3}/$_4$ cup chopped seeded tomato (about
  1 medium)
2 tablespoons sliced green onion tops

Prepare Chipotle Sauce as directed; pour into 1-cup microwavable measure. Arrange turkey slices on microwavable dinner plate. Cover with waxed paper and microwave on medium-high (70%) 4 minutes; rotate plate ^{1}/$_2$ turn. Microwave until no longer pink, 4 to 6 minutes longer. Microwave Chipotle Sauce uncovered on high, stirring every 15 seconds, until hot, about 1^1/$_2$ minutes. Arrange turkey on serving plate; top with sauce. Sprinkle with tomato and green onion tops.

Note: If turkey slices are too thick, pound between plastic wrap or waxed paper until ^{1}/$_4$ to ^{1}/$_2$ inch thick.

CHIPOTLE SAUCE

^{1}/$_2$ cup nonfat plain yogurt
2 tablespoons chopped green onions
1 to 2 tablespoons chopped, seeded,
  drained, canned chipotle chilies in
  adobo sauce
2 tablespoons creamy peanut butter
^{1}/$_8$ teaspoon salt

Place all ingredients in blender container. Cover and blend on medium speed until well blended, about 20 seconds.

Southwestern Stuffed Peppers

6 SERVINGS; 175 CALORIES PER SERVING

3 large bell peppers (green, red, purple or yellow)
½ pound ground turkey, cooked and drained
1 cup cooked rice
¼ cup chopped onion (about 1 small)
1 teaspoon ground cumin
½ teaspoon salt
¼ teaspoon pepper
2 eggs
2 cloves garlic, finely chopped
1 can (4 ounces) chopped green chilies
1 jar (2 ounces) diced pimientos, drained
½ cup shredded Monterey Jack cheese (2 ounces)

Cut bell peppers lengthwise into halves. Remove seeds and membranes; rinse. Cook conventionally 2 minutes in enough boiling water to cover; drain. Mix remaining ingredients except cheese; loosely stuff each pepper half. Arrange stuffed peppers in rectangular microwavable baking dish, 12 × 7½ × 2 inches. Cover with vented plastic wrap and microwave on high 6 minutes; rotate dish ½ turn. Sprinkle with cheese. Microwave uncovered until rice mixture is hot and cheese is melted, 1 to 3 minutes longer.

Turkey and Wild Rice Soup

6 SERVINGS; 115 CALORIES PER SERVING

½ cup uncooked wild rice
3 cups hot water
1 tablespoon instant chicken bouillon (dry)
2 turkey drumsticks (about 1½ pounds)
2 medium stalks celery (with leaves), sliced
1 medium onion, chopped
2 bay leaves
1 can (16 ounces) stewed tomatoes

Mix all ingredients in 3-quart microwavable casserole. Cover tightly and microwave on high, turning drumsticks over every 10 minutes, until turkey is done, 30 to 40 minutes. Remove turkey; cool about 5 minutes.

Cover wild rice mixture tightly and microwave until wild rice is tender, 8 to 10 minutes longer. Remove skin and bones from turkey; cut turkey into bite-size pieces. Stir turkey into soup. Cover tightly and microwave until hot, 2 to 3 minutes. Remove bay leaves.

Turkey Chili

½ cup chopped green bell pepper

¼ cup chopped onion (about 1 small)

2 cloves garlic, finely chopped

2 teaspoons olive or vegetable oil

3 cups cut-up cooked turkey or chicken

½ cup water

1 tablespoon snipped fresh oregano leaves
  or 1 teaspoon dried oregano leaves

1 tablespoon chili powder

1 teaspoon ground cumin

½ teaspoon salt

1 can (16 ounces) whole tomatoes,
  undrained

1 package (10 ounces) frozen mixed
  vegetables

2 cups ½-inch slices zucchini (about
  2 medium)

Place bell pepper, onion, garlic and oil in 3-quart microwavable casserole. Cover tightly and microwave on high 3 minutes. Stir in remaining ingredients except frozen vegetables and zucchini; break up tomatoes. Cover and microwave 15 minutes. Stir in frozen vegetables; cover and microwave 10 minutes. Stir in zucchini; cover and microwave until zucchini is crisp-tender, 3 to 6 minutes longer.

Following pages: Southwestern Stuffed Peppers

· 3 ·

QUICK AND EASY MEATS

Beef and Eggplant

6 SERVINGS; 280 CALORIES PER SERVING

*1-pound beef round steak, ½ inch thick,
cut into 1½ × 1¼-inch strips*

1 tablespoon vegetable oil

1 can (8 ounces) tomato sauce

1 can (6 ounces) tomato paste

¼ cup water

1 medium onion, chopped (about ½ cup)

*1 medium green pepper, chopped (about
1 cup)*

1 teaspoon salt

1 teaspoon garlic salt

*1 tablespoon snipped fresh oregano leaves
or 1 teaspoon dried oregano leaves*

*1½ teaspoons snipped fresh basil leaves
or ½ teaspoon dried basil leaves*

*1 package (9 ounces) frozen Italian green
beans*

*1 medium eggplant (about 1½ pounds),
pared and cut into ¼-inch slices*

*1 cup shredded mozzarella cheese (about
4 ounces)*

¼ cup grated Parmesan cheese

Place beef round steak strips and oil in 2-quart microwavable casserole. Cover tightly and microwave on medium (50%) 6 minutes; stir. Cover and microwave until beef is brown, 6 to 11 minutes longer. Stir in tomato sauce, tomato paste, ¼ cup water, the onion, green pepper, salt, garlic salt, oregano and basil. Cover tightly and microwave on high 5 minutes; stir. Cover tightly and microwave on medium (50%) 20 minutes.

Rinse frozen beans under running cold water to separate. Layer half each of the eggplant slices, beans and beef mixture in ungreased 2-quart casserole; repeat. Cover tightly and microwave on medium (50%) until beans and eggplant are tender, 24 to 30 minutes. Sprinkle casserole with cheeses. Cover and let stand 10 minutes before serving.

Beef Steaks with Mushrooms

4 SERVINGS; 235 CALORIES PER SERVING

1 teaspoon bottled brown bouquet sauce
1 tablespoon water
4 beef cubed steaks (3 to 4 ounces each)
½ teaspoon salt
¼ teaspoon lemon pepper
1 can (4 ounces) sliced mushrooms,
   drained
¼ cup chopped green pepper
¼ cup chopped onion (about 1 small)
2 tablespoons dry white wine

Mix bouquet sauce and water; brush both sides of beef cubed steaks. Arrange steaks in microwavable baking dish, 8 × 8 × 2 inches. Sprinkle with salt and lemon pepper. Top with mushrooms, green pepper and onion; drizzle with wine. Cover with waxed paper and microwave on high 5 minutes; rotate baking dish ½ turn. Microwave until steaks are tender and no longer pink, 4 to 6 minutes longer. Let stand 5 minutes.

Oriental Beef and Pea Pods

6 SERVINGS; 280 CALORIES PER SERVING

1 small head cauliflower
1 green pepper, cut into strips
1 pound beef round steak or tenderloin
   tip, cut into paper-thin strips, about
   3 inches long
1 clove garlic, minced
1 medium onion, chopped
2 tablespoons soy sauce
1 package (6 ounces) frozen pea pods
2 cups water
¼ cup cornstarch
4 teaspoons instant beef bouillon
½ teaspoon sugar
3 cups hot cooked rice

Break cauliflower into flowerets; cut each into ¼-inch slices. Combine cauliflower, green pepper, beef, garlic and onion in 2-quart microwavable casserole. Drizzle with soy sauce; stir lightly to coat evenly. Cover and microwave on high 6 minutes; stir. Cover and microwave until meat is no longer pink, 3 to 5 minutes.

Add frozen pea pods. Cover and microwave until pea pods are thawed, 2 to 3 minutes.

Mix water, cornstarch, bouillon (dry) and sugar in 4-cup microwavable glass measure. Stir in juices from meat. Microwave uncovered on high 2½ minutes; stir. Microwave to boiling, 2 to 3 minutes. Stir into meat mixture. Serve over rice.

Following pages: Oriental Beef and Pea Pods

Savory Beef Ragout

6 SERVINGS; 280 CALORIES PER SERVING

1½ pounds beef chuck or bottom round,
  cut into ½-inch pieces
1½ cups cold water
¼ cup all-purpose flour
1 can (about 8½ ounces) stewed tomatoes
3 sprigs parsley
2 teaspoons salt
1½ teaspoons snipped fresh thyme leaves
  or ½ teaspoon dried thyme leaves
¾ teaspoon snipped fresh sage leaves or
  ¼ teaspoon dried sage leaves
¼ teaspoon pepper
1 bay leaf
1 clove garlic, finely chopped
6 small onions
3 large carrots, cut diagonally into
  ½-inch slices (about 2 cups)
1 package (10 ounces) frozen lima beans,
  broken apart

Place beef pieces in 3-quart microwavable casserole. Cover tightly and microwave on high 7 minutes; stir. Cover tightly and microwave until beef is no longer pink, 4 to 7 minutes; drain, reserving liquid. Remove beef.

If necessary, add enough water to reserved liquid to measure 1 cup; return to casserole. Mix ½ cup cold water and the flour; stir into casserole. Microwave uncovered, stirring every minute, until thickened, 3 to 4 minutes. Stir in beef, tomatoes, parsley, salt, thyme, sage, pepper, bay leaf and garlic. Cover tightly and microwave until boiling, 6 to 10 minutes; stir. Cover tightly and microwave on medium (50%) 30 minutes; add onions and carrots. Cover tightly and microwave 10 minutes; stir. Cover and microwave until beef and vegetables are tender, 30 to 35 minutes longer. Stir in frozen beans; cover tightly and microwave until beans are tender, 10 to 12 minutes. Remove bay leaf.

Quick Beef Casserole

1½ cups cut-up cooked beef
1½ cups uncooked elbow macaroni (about
    6 ounces)
1 cup sliced celery (about 2 medium
    stalks)
½ cup skim milk
¼ cup chopped onion (about 1 small)
1 tablespoon snipped fresh basil leaves
    or 1½ teaspoons dried basil leaves
½ teaspoon garlic powder
⅛ teaspoon pepper
1 can (8 ounces) mushroom stems and
    pieces, undrained
1 can (8 ounces) tomato sauce

Mix all ingredients in 3-quart microwavable casserole; pour ½ cup water over top. Cover tightly and microwave on high, stirring every 6 minutes, until macaroni is tender, 15 to 18 minutes. Let stand covered 5 minutes.

Stuffed Bell Peppers

6 large green, red or yellow peppers
1 pound ground beef
2 tablespoons chopped onion
1 cup cooked rice
1 teaspoon salt
⅛ teaspoon garlic salt
1 can (15 ounces) tomato sauce
¾ cup shredded mozzarella cheese
    (3 ounces)

Cut thin slice from stem end of each pepper. Remove seeds and membranes; rinse peppers. Place peppers, cut sides up, in microwavable pie plate, 9 × 1¼ inches or 10 × 1½ inches. Cover with vented plastic wrap and microwave on high until hot, 3 to 3½ minutes.

Mix uncooked ground beef, onion, cooked rice, salt, garlic salt and 1 cup of the tomato sauce. Stuff each pepper with about ½ cup beef mixture. Pour remaining sauce over peppers. Cover with vented plastic wrap and microwave 6 minutes; rotate plate ¼ turn. Microwave until mixture is done, 6 to 7 minutes longer. Sprinkle with cheese.

Oriental Vegetable Meat Roll

6 SERVINGS; 235 CALORIES PER SERVING

1 pound lean ground beef
1 cup soft whole wheat bread crumbs
  (about 2 slices)
1 egg
⅓ cup coarsely chopped green onions
  (with tops)
2 tablespoons soy sauce
1 teaspoon ground ginger
¼ teaspoon pepper
1 can (8 ounces) water chestnuts, chopped
1 can (2.5 ounces) mushroom stems and
  pieces, drained
1 jar (2 ounces) diced pimientos, drained

Mix all ingredients except water chestnuts, mushrooms and pimientos. Shape mixture into 12 × 10-inch rectangle on waxed paper. Mix remaining ingredients. Spread over beef mixture to within 1 inch of edges; press into beef mixture. Roll up, beginning at narrow end, using waxed paper to help roll. Pinch edges and ends to seal.

Place roll, seam side down, on microwavable rack in microwavable dish. Cover with waxed paper and microwave on medium-high (70%) 10 minutes; rotate dish ½ turn. Microwave until done, 12 to 15 minutes longer. Let stand covered 5 minutes.

Meatballs in Dijon Sauce

6 SERVINGS; 210 CALORIES PER SERVING

1 pound lean ground beef
1 slice whole wheat bread, crumbled
¼ cup finely chopped onion (about
  1 small)
1 tablespoon Dijon-style mustard
¼ teaspoon salt
¼ teaspoon pepper
Dijon Sauce (page 47)

Mix all ingredients except Dijon Sauce. Shape into twenty-four 1¼-inch meatballs. Place in rectangular microwavable dish, 12 × 7½ × 2 inches. Cover with waxed paper and microwave on high 3 minutes; rearrange meatballs. Cover and microwave until no longer pink inside, 4 to 6 minutes longer. Let stand covered 3 minutes; drain. Stir in sauce.

DIJON SAUCE

3 tablespoons all-purpose flour
1 tablespoon cornstarch
1½ teaspoons instant beef bouillon
1 cup water
1 cup skim milk
3 tablespoons finely snipped chives
2 tablespoons Dijon-style mustard
¼ teaspoon pepper
1 teaspoon lemon juice

Mix all ingredients for Dijon Sauce in 2-quart microwavable casserole. Microwave uncovered, stirring every minute until thickened, 4 to 6 minutes.

Stuffed Cabbage Leaves

6 SERVINGS; 280 CALORIES PER SERVING

12 cabbage leaves
¼ cup cold water
1 pound lean hamburger
½ cup instant rice
1 medium onion, chopped
1 can (4 ounces) mushroom stems and
   pieces, with liquid
1 teaspoon salt
⅛ teaspoon garlic salt
⅛ teaspoon pepper
1 can (15 ounces) tomato sauce
1 teaspoon sugar
½ teaspoon lemon juice
1 tablespoon cornstarch
1 tablespoon cold water

Cover and microwave cabbage leaves and ¼ cup cold water in 3-quart microwavable casserole on high until limp, 4 to 5 minutes; drain.

Mix hamburger, rice, onion, mushrooms (with liquid), salt, garlic salt, pepper and ½ cup of the tomato sauce. Place about ⅓ cup meat mixture at stem end of each cabbage leaf. Roll leaf around meat mixture, tucking in sides. Place cabbage rolls seam sides down in 3-quart casserole.

Mix remaining tomato sauce, the sugar and lemon juice. Blend cornstarch and 1 tablespoon cold water; stir into tomato sauce mixture. Pour over cabbage rolls. Cover and microwave on high 7 minutes; turn casserole ¼ turn. Microwave until meat is done, 8 to 9 minutes. Let stand 1 minute. Remove cabbage rolls to platter. Stir sauce in casserole with fork; pour over cabbage rolls.

Beef and Bulgur Casserole

8 SERVINGS; 300 CALORIES PER SERVING

1½ pounds lean ground beef
1 cup chopped onion (about 1 large)
2 cups chopped tomatoes
2 cups water
1 cup uncooked bulgur (cracked wheat)
3 tablespoons snipped parsley
2 teaspoons instant beef bouillon (dry)
1½ teaspoons salt
1½ teaspoons snipped fresh oregano
   leaves or ½ teaspoon dried oregano
   leaves
¼ teaspoon instant minced garlic
¼ teaspoon pepper
¼ cup grated Parmesan cheese

Crumble ground beef into 3-quart microwavable casserole; add onion. Cover loosely and microwave on high 5 minutes; break up and stir. Cover and microwave until very little pink remains, 4 to 6 minutes longer; drain. Stir in remaining ingredients except cheese. Cover tightly and microwave 10 minutes; stir. Cover and microwave until bulgur is tender, 10 to 15 minutes longer. Stir in cheese. Sprinkle with snipped parsley, if desired.

Beef-Vegetable Soup

6 SERVINGS; 230 CALORIES PER SERVING

1 pound lean ground beef
½ cup chopped onion (about 1 medium)
⅔ cup chopped carrot (about 1 large)
⅔ cup chopped celery
⅔ cup ½-inch pieces potato
¼ cup water
1½ teaspoons salt
1 teaspoon bottled brown bouquet sauce
¼ teaspoon pepper
½ teaspoon snipped fresh basil leaves or
   ⅛ teaspoon dried basil leaves
1 bay leaf
1¾ cups hot water
1 can (16 ounces) whole tomatoes

Crumble ground beef into 3-quart microwavable casserole; add onion. Cover loosely and microwave on high 3 minutes; break up and stir. Cover and microwave until very little pink remains in beef, 2 to 3 minutes longer; drain.

Stir in remaining ingredients except 1¾ cups water and tomatoes. Cover tightly and microwave on high 5 minutes; stir. Cover and microwave until vegetables are tender, 4 to 6 minutes longer.

Stir water and tomatoes (with liquid) into beef mixture; break up tomatoes with fork. Cover tightly and microwave on high 5 minutes; stir. Cover and microwave to boiling, 4 to 6 minutes longer. Remove bay leaf.

Veal with Sour Cream

4 SERVINGS; 300 CALORIES PER SERVING

1 medium onion, finely chopped
2 tablespoons margarine or butter
1 can (4 ounces) mushroom stems and
   pieces, drained
1 teaspoon instant chicken bouillon
1/3 cup boiling water
1/2 teaspoon paprika
1/4 teaspoon salt
3/4 teaspoon snipped fresh dill or
   1/4 teaspoon dried dill weed
1/8 teaspoon pepper
2 one-inch strips lemon peel
1 pound veal shoulder steak, about 1/2
   inch thick, cut into serving pieces
1/4 cup cold water
1 1/2 teaspoons cornstarch
1/2 cup dairy sour cream

Place onion and margarine in 4-cup microwavable measure. Microwave uncovered on high until onion is tender, 2 to 3 minutes. Stir in mushrooms, bouillon (dry), 1/3 cup hot water, the paprika, salt, dill, pepper and lemon peel. Place veal in rectangular microwavable dish, 10 × 6 × 1 1/2 inches. Pour onion mixture over veal. Cover tightly and microwave on medium (50%) 10 minutes; rotate dish 1/2 turn. Microwave until veal is no longer pink, 4 to 7 minutes longer. Remove veal to warm platter.

Mix cold water and 1 tablespoon cornstarch; stir into onion mixture gradually. Stir in sour cream. Microwave uncovered on high, stirring every minute, until thickened, 2 to 4 minutes. Pour over veal.

Greek-style Lamb with Orzo

4 SERVINGS; 210 CALORIES PER SERVING

1 pound ground lamb or beef
1 can (16 ounces) stewed tomatoes
1 stalk celery, cut into 1/2-inch pieces
1/2 cup orzo
1/2 teaspoon salt
1/4 teaspoon ground red pepper
Plain yogurt

Crumble ground lamb into 2-quart microwavable casserole. Cover with waxed paper and microwave on high 3 minutes; stir. Cover with waxed paper and microwave until lamb is no longer pink, 2 to 3 minutes longer; drain.

Stir in remaining ingredients except yogurt. Cover tightly and microwave 4 minutes; stir. Cover tightly and microwave, stirring every 2 minutes, until orzo is tender, 8 to 10 minutes longer. Serve with yogurt.

Lamb Patties with Fresh Mint Sauce

4 SERVINGS; 260 CALORIES PER SERVING

Fresh Mint Sauce (below)
1 pound lean ground lamb
⅔ cup soft bread crumbs
⅓ cup dry red wine
½ teaspoon salt
*¾ teaspoon snipped fresh rosemary leaves
  or ¼ teaspoon dried rosemary leaves,
  crushed*
2 small cloves garlic, finely chopped

Prepare Fresh Mint Sauce. Mix remaining ingredients. Shape lamb mixture into 4 patties, each about 1 inch thick. Place patties on microwavable rack in microwavable dish. Cover with vented plastic wrap and microwave on high 3 minutes; rotate dish ½ turn. Microwave until patties are almost done, 3 to 4 minutes longer. Let stand covered 3 minutes. Serve with Fresh Mint Sauce. Garnish with mint leaves and sliced kiwifruit, if desired.

FRESH MINT SAUCE

*¼ cup mashed pared kiwifruit (about
  1 medium)*
*1 tablespoon snipped fresh mint leaves or
  ½ teaspoon dried mint leaves, crushed*
2 teaspoons sugar
2 teaspoons lime juice

Mix all ingredients.

Lamb Patties with Summer Squash

4 SERVINGS; 175 CALORIES PER SERVING

1 pound ground lamb
½ teaspoon garlic salt
¼ teaspoon pepper
2 small onions, cut into fourths
1 small green pepper, sliced
*1 small summer squash, cut into ½-inch
  slices*
*1 tablespoon snipped fresh marjoram
  leaves or 1 teaspoon dried marjoram leaves*

Mix lamb, garlic salt and pepper. Shape into 4 patties, each about ½ inch thick. Arrange on microwavable rack in microwavable dish. Cover with waxed paper and microwave on high 4 minutes.

Arrange vegetables on and around lamb; sprinkle with marjoram. Cover with waxed paper and microwave 4 minutes; rotate rack ½ turn. Microwave until vegetables are crisp-tender and lamb is done, 3 to 5 minutes longer.

Oriental Pork

1 pound boneless fresh pork shoulder,
cut into ¹/₄-inch strips
¹/₂ cup water
¹/₂ cup orange juice
¹/₄ teaspoon salt
¹/₈ teaspoon pepper
3 tablespoons soy sauce
1 can (8 ounces) sliced water chestnuts,
drained
1 can (16 ounces) bean sprouts, drained
2 cups thinly sliced Chinese cabbage
1 tablespoon cornstarch
1 tablespoon cold water
2 tablespoons chopped green onions

Mix pork, ¹/₂ cup water, the orange juice, salt, pepper and soy sauce in 2-quart microwavable casserole. Cover and microwave on medium (50%) until pork is tender, 16 to 20 minutes, stirring every 3 minutes.

Stir in water chestnuts, bean sprouts and cabbage. Cover and microwave on high until cabbage is crisp-tender, 3 to 4 minutes.

Blend cornstarch and 1 tablespoon water in 4-cup microwavable glass measure. Drain juices from meat mixture into cornstarch mixture; stir well. Microwave uncovered on high until mixture boils and thickens, 3 to 4 minutes, stirring every minute. Pour over meat and vegetables. Sprinkle with onions.

Pineapple Pork Chops

4 lean pork loin or rib chops, about
¹/₂ inch thick
Salt
1 can (8 ounces) pineapple slices in juice,
drained (reserve juice)
2 tablespoons packed brown sugar
¹/₄ teaspoon ground nutmeg

Trim fat from pork chops. Lightly sprinkle both sides of pork with salt. Arrange pork with narrow ends toward center, in square microwavable dish, 8 × 8 × 2 inches. Mix 2 tablespoons of the reserved pineapple juice with brown sugar and nutmeg; spoon half of the mixture over pork. Cover with vented plastic wrap and microwave on medium (50%) 10 minutes. Arrange pineapple slices over pork; spoon remaining mixture over pineapple and pork. Cover and rotate dish ¹/₂ turn. Microwave until pork is done, 10 to 15 minutes longer. Let stand covered about 3 minutes. Garnish with snipped chives, if desired.

Following pages: Lamb Patties with Fresh Mint Sauce

Pork Chops with Rhubarb Sauce

4 SERVINGS; 285 CALORIES PER SERVING

4 lean rib or loin pork chops, about
   1/2 inch thick
1 tablespoon snipped fresh rosemary
   leaves or 1 teaspoon dried rosemary
   leaves
1/2 teaspoon salt
1/4 teaspoon pepper
3 tablespoons unsweetened apple juice
1 tablespoon packed brown sugar
2 tablespoons cold water
1 tablespoon cornstarch
2 cups chopped rhubarb (about
   6 medium stalks)

Trim fat from pork chops. Mix rosemary, salt and pepper; rub over pork. Arrange pork with narrow ends toward center, in square microwavable dish, 8 × 8 × 2 inches. Cover with vented plastic wrap and microwave on medium (50%), rotating dish 1/4 turn every 5 minutes until pork is done, 20 to 23 minutes. Let stand covered 5 minutes.

Mix apple juice, brown sugar, water and cornstarch in 4-cup microwavable measure; stir in rhubarb. Cover with vented plastic wrap and microwave on high, stirring every 2 minutes, until thickened, 4 to 6 minutes. Serve with pork chops.

Ginger Pork on Pineapple

6 SERVINGS; 260 CALORIES PER SERVING

1 pineapple
1 pound lean ground pork
1/4 cup chopped onion (about 1 small)
1 tablespoon packed brown sugar
1 tablespoon vinegar
1 teaspoon ground ginger
1/2 teaspoon salt
1/4 teaspoon pepper
1 medium green bell pepper, cut into
   1-inch pieces
1 can (8 ounces) tomato sauce
1 can (8 ounces) sliced water chestnuts,
   drained

Pare pineapple; cut crosswise into 6 slices, about 1 inch thick. Arrange pineapple slices on deep round microwavable platter. Cover pineapple with waxed paper.

Crumble pork and onion in 2-quart microwavable casserole. Cover tightly and microwave on high 3 minutes; stir. Cover and microwave until pork is done, 3 to 5 minutes longer; drain. Stir in remaining ingredients. Cover and microwave 5 minutes; stir. Cover and microwave until bell pepper is crisp-tender, 3 to 5 minutes longer. Let stand covered 5 minutes. Microwave pineapple until hot, about 4 minutes. Serve pork mixture on pineapple slices.

Festive Ham

4½- to 5-pound fully cooked boneless smoked ham, cut into ¼-inch slices and tied
3 tablespoons corn syrup
2 tablespoons brown sugar
1 teaspoon prepared mustard
Mustard Sauce (below)

Place ham fat side down in round microwavable dish, 8 × 1½ inches. Cover tightly and microwave on medium (50%) 25 minutes; turn ham fat side up. Cover ham tightly and microwave until hot, 18 to 25 minutes. Mix corn syrup, brown sugar and mustard; brush on ham. Cover with aluminum foil and let stand 10 minutes. Serve with Mustard Sauce.

MUSTARD SAUCE

1 tablespoon margarine or butter
1 tablespoon flour
½ teaspoon salt
¼ teaspoon pepper
1 cup milk
3 tablespoons prepared mustard
1 tablespoon prepared horseradish

Place margarine in 4-cup microwavable measure. Microwave uncovered on high until melted, 15 to 30 seconds. Stir in flour, salt, pepper and milk. Microwave, stirring every minute, until thickened, 2 to 3 minutes. Stir in mustard and horseradish. Microwave until hot, 30 to 60 seconds longer.

Following pages: Pork Chops with Rhubarb Sauce

Ham- and Swiss-topped Potatoes   6 SERVINGS; 220 CALORIES PER SERVING

3 medium baking potatoes
2 tablespoons cornstarch
1³/₄ cups skim milk
1 tablespoon Dijon-style mustard
¼ teaspoon pepper
½ cup shredded Swiss cheese (2 ounces)
2 cups cut-up fully cooked smoked extra
   lean ham (about 8 ounces)
1 package (10 ounces) frozen asparagus
   cuts, thawed and drained

Arrange potatoes about 2 inches apart in circle in microwave. Microwave uncovered on high until tender, 10 to 13 minutes. Let stand 5 minutes. Mix cornstarch and milk in 2-quart microwavable casserole. Microwave uncovered, stirring every minute, until thickened, 4 to 6 minutes. Stir in mustard, pepper and cheese until cheese is melted. Stir in ham and asparagus. Microwave until heated through, 4 to 6 minutes.

To serve, cut potatoes lengthwise into halves. Make ½-inch deep cuts lengthwise and crosswise at ½-inch intervals in cut sides of potatoes. Push ends to open potato. Serve sauce over potato halves.

· 4 ·

SAUCY FISH

Halibut Steaks with Wine

3 SERVINGS; 180 CALORIES PER SERVING

³/₄ pound halibut steaks
2 tablespoons dry white wine
¹/₄ teaspoon salt
³/₄ teaspoon snipped fresh oregano leaves
  or ¹/₄ teaspoon dried oregano leaves
1 tablespoon dry bread crumbs
1 tablespoon grated Parmesan cheese
1 tablespoon margarine or butter, melted
1 green onion (with top), finely chopped

Arrange fish with thickest parts to outside edge in microwavable dish, 10 × 6 × 2 inches. Sprinkle with wine, salt and oregano. Cover tightly and microwave on high 3 minutes; drain.

Sprinkle fish with bread crumbs and cheese; drizzle with margarine. Rotate baking dish ½ turn. Microwave uncovered on high until small ends of fish flake easily with fork, 2 to 4 minutes. Let stand 3 minutes. (Fish will continue to cook while standing.) Remove fish to platter. Sprinkle with onion.

Cold Poached Salmon

8 SERVINGS; 45 CALORIES PER SERVING

4 salmon steaks, 1 inch thick (about
   2 pounds)
1 small onion, sliced
1 stalk celery (with leaves), chopped
4 parsley sprigs
1 teaspoon salt
5 peppercorns
1 bay leaf
¾ teaspoon snipped fresh thyme leaves
   or ¼ teaspoon dried thyme leaves
¾ teaspoon snipped fresh tarragon leaves
   or ¼ teaspoon dried tarragon leaves
1 cup water
½ cup dry white wine
Green Sauce (below)

Rinse fish steaks under gently running cold water. Place fish in ungreased microwavable dish, 12 × 7½ × 2 inches. Place onion, celery, parsley, salt, peppercorns, bay leaf, thyme and tarragon on fish. Pour 1 cup water and the cup wine over fish. Cover tightly and microwave on high 3 minutes; rotate dish ½ turn. Microwave until small ends of fish flake easily with fork, 5 to 7 minutes. Let stand 3 minutes. Carefully remove fish with slotted spoon; place on wire rack to drain. Carefully remove skin; cut fish lengthwise into halves. Cover and refrigerate until cold, at least 4 hours. Prepare Green Sauce; serve with fish.

GREEN SAUCE

1 cup parsley sprigs
1½ cups creamed cottage cheese (large
   curd)
1 tablespoon lemon juice
1 tablespoon milk
1½ teaspoons snipped fresh basil leaves
   or ½ teaspoon dried basil leaves
½ teaspoon salt
⅛ teaspoon pepper
4 to 6 drops red pepper sauce

Place all ingredients in blender container. Cover and blend on high speed, stopping blender occasionally to scrape sides, until smooth, about 3 minutes.

Marinated Tarragon Salmon

2 salmon steaks, about 1 inch thick
1/4 teaspoon salt
3/4 teaspoon snipped fresh dill or
   1/4 teaspoon dried dill weed
3 slices lemon
1 small onion, thinly sliced
1/4 cup wine vinegar
3/4 teaspoon snipped fresh tarragon leaves
   or 1/4 teaspoon dried tarragon leaves
1 small cucumber
1/2 cup plain yogurt
1/4 teaspoon salt
1/4 teaspoon snipped fresh dill or
   1/8 teaspoon dried dill weed
Lettuce leaves
2 medium tomatoes, sliced

Place salmon in square microwavable dish, 8 × 8 × 2 inches. Sprinkle with 1/4 teaspoon salt and 3/4 teaspoon dill. Arrange lemon slices on top. Cover tightly and microwave on high 3 minutes; rotate dish 1/2 turn. Microwave until small ends of fish flake easily with fork, 3 to 6 minutes longer. Let stand covered 3 minutes; drain. Discard lemon slices.

Carefully remove skin from salmon. Place salmon in shallow glass or plastic dish; arrange onion on fish. Mix vinegar and tarragon; drizzle over onion and fish. Cover and refrigerate, spooning vinegar mixture over salmon 2 or 3 times, at least 8 hours but no longer than 24 hours.

About 20 minutes before serving, cut cucumber lengthwise into halves; remove seeds. Cut both halves crosswise into thin slices. Mix cucumber, yogurt, 1/4 teaspoon salt and 1/4 teaspoon dill. Place salmon on lettuce leaves; arrange onion and tomatoes around fish. Drizzle any remaining marinade over fish. Serve with cucumber mixture. Garnish with fresh dill or watercress, if desired.

Following pages: Marinated Tarragon Salmon, left, and Salmon Steak with Asparagus and Peas, right (page 79)

Sweet and Sour Fish

4 SERVINGS; 210 CALORIES PER SERVING

1 can (8 ounces) pineapple chunks in
    juice
1/4 cup sugar
2 tablespoons cornstarch
1/4 cup vinegar
1 teaspoon soy sauce
1/4 teaspoon salt
1 small clove garlic, finely chopped
1 small green pepper, cut into 1/2-inch
    strips
2 fish steaks (about 3/4 pound)
1 tomato, cut into 8 wedges

Drain pineapple; reserve juice. Add enough water to reserved juice to measure 1 cup. Mix sugar and cornstarch in 4-cup microwavable measure. Stir in pineapple juice, vinegar, soy sauce, 1/4 teaspoon salt and the garlic. Microwave uncovered on high, stirring every minute, until mixture thickens and boils, 3 to 5 minutes. Stir in pineapple chunks and green pepper.

Place fish steaks in square microwavable dish, 8 × 8 × 2 inches. Pour pineapple mixture over fish. Cover tightly and microwave 4 minutes; rotate dish 1/2 turn. Microwave until fish flakes easily with fork, 2 to 4 minutes longer. Add tomato wedges. Let stand covered 3 minutes.

Salmon Steaks with Lemon

4 SERVINGS; 200 CALORIES PER SERVING

2 tablespoons margarine or butter
2 tablespoons lemon juice
4 salmon or halibut steaks, 3/4 inch thick
1 teaspoon onion salt
1/4 teaspoon pepper
1 1/2 teaspoons fresh snipped marjoram or
    thyme leaves or 1/2 teaspoon dried
    marjoram or thyme leaves
Paprika
Lemon wedges

Place margarine and lemon juice in square microwavable dish, 8 × 8 × 2 inches. Microwave uncovered on high until margarine is melted, 45 to 60 seconds; stir. Place salmon steaks in dish with thickest parts to outside edges; turn to coat both sides with lemon butter. Sprinkle with onion salt, pepper and marjoram. Cover tightly and microwave 4 minutes; spoon lemon butter over salmon and rotate dish 1/2 turn. Cover tightly and microwave until small ends of salmon flake easily with fork, 2 to 5 minutes longer. Let stand 3 minutes. Sprinkle with paprika; serve with lemon wedges.

Marinated Shark Steaks

4 SERVINGS; 125 CALORIES PER SERVING

1 pound shark or lean fish steaks,
¾ inch thick
¼ cup orange juice
2 tablespoons snipped parsley
2 tablespoons chili sauce
1 tablespoon snipped fresh basil leaves
or 1 teaspoon dried basil leaves
1 tablespoon soy sauce
1 clove garlic, finely chopped
½ lemon, cut into 4 wedges

Arrange fish, thickest parts to outside edges, in square microwavable dish, 8 × 8 × 2 inches. Mix remaining ingredients; pour over fish. Cover and refrigerate at least 1 hour but no longer than 6 hours, turning once. Microwave on high 4 minutes; rotate dish ½ turn. Microwave until fish flakes easily with fork, 2 to 4 minutes longer. Let stand covered 3 minutes. Serve with lemon wedges.

Monterey Fish Steaks

6 SERVINGS; 230 CALORIES PER SERVING

1½ pounds swordfish, halibut or salmon
steaks, each ¾ to 1 inch thick
1 teaspoon salt
¼ teaspoon pepper
2 tablespoons margarine or butter, melted
1 tablespoon snipped fresh chervil leaves
or 1 teaspoon dried chervil leaves
1 tablespoon lemon juice
Avocado Sauce (below)
Lemon wedges

Sprinkle fish steaks with salt and pepper. Arrange fish, with thickest parts to outside edges, in square microwavable dish, 8 × 8 × 2 inches.

Mix margarine, chervil and lemon juice; drizzle over fish. Cover tightly and microwave on high 4 minutes; rotate dish ½ turn. Microwave until fish flakes easily with fork, 4 to 7 minutes longer. Let stand covered 3 minutes. Cut into serving pieces. Serve with Avocado Sauce and lemon wedges.

AVOCADO SAUCE

1 small avocado, peeled and cut up
⅓ cup dairy sour cream
1 teaspoon lemon juice
¼ teaspoon salt
Few drops red pepper sauce

Beat all ingredients with hand beater until mixture is smooth.

Following pages: Marinated Shark Steaks

Fish Fillets with Grapes

5 SERVINGS; 190 CALORIES PER SERVING

2 green onions (with tops), finely chopped
1 pound sole fillets, cut into 5 serving
  pieces
1/2 teaspoon salt
1/8 teaspoon pepper
1/3 cup dry white wine
2 teaspoons lemon juice
1 tablespoon margarine or butter
1 tablespoon all-purpose flour
2 tablespoons milk
2 tablespoons dry white wine
1 cup seedless green grapes or 1 can
  (8 ounces) green grapes, drained

Sprinkle green onions in 9-inch microwavable pie plate. Sprinkle fish with salt and pepper. Fold fillets in half; arrange in circle on onions with folded sides to outside edge in pie plate. Add 1/3 cup wine and the lemon juice. Cover tightly and microwave on high 3 minutes; rotate pie plate 1/2 turn. Microwave until fish flakes easily with fork, 2 to 4 minutes longer. Remove fish to platter; keep warm. Reserve liquid.

Place 1 tablespoon margarine in 4-cup microwavable measure. Microwave uncovered on high until melted, 15 to 30 seconds. Stir in flour; add milk, 2 tablespoons wine and the liquid from fish. Microwave uncovered, stirring every minute until thickened, 3 to 4 minutes; stir in grapes. Spoon sauce over fish. Sprinkle with paprika, if desired.

Sole Gratin

4 SERVINGS; 215 CALORIES PER SERVING

3 cups sliced mushrooms (about 8 ounces)
1/2 teaspoon salt
1/4 teaspoon pepper
1 pound sole or lean fish fillets
1/4 cup sliced green onions (with tops)
3 tablespoons snipped fresh cilantro or
  1 tablespoon dried cilantro leaves
1/4 cup dry white wine
1/3 cup coarsely crushed zwieback
2 tablespoons reduced-calorie margarine,
  melted

Layer mushrooms in rectangular microwavable dish, 12 × 7½ × 2 inches; sprinkle with half of the salt and half of the pepper. Arrange fish, thickest parts to outside edges, on top; sprinkle with remaining salt and pepper, the green onions and cilantro. Pour wine around fish. Cover with vented plastic wrap and microwave on high 4 minutes; rotate dish 1/2 turn. Uncover and microwave until fish flakes easily with fork, 2 to 4 minutes longer. Mix zwieback and margarine; sprinkle evenly over fish.

Flounder with Mushrooms and Wine

4 SERVINGS; 210 CALORIES PER SERVING

1 pound flounder or lean fish fillets
1/2 teaspoon paprika
1/4 teaspoon salt
1/8 teaspoon pepper
1 1/2 cups sliced mushrooms (about
   4 ounces)
1/3 cup sliced leeks
1 tablespoon reduced-calorie margarine
1/4 cup dry white wine
1/4 cup sliced almonds
1 tablespoon grated Parmesan cheese

If fish fillets are large, cut into 4 serving pieces. Arrange fish, thickest parts to outside edges, in square microwavable dish, 8 × 8 × 2 inches. Sprinkle with paprika, salt and pepper.

Place mushrooms, leeks and margarine in 1-quart microwavable casserole. Cover tightly and microwave on high 2 minutes; stir and drain. Spoon mushroom mixture over fish; pour wine over top. Cover with vented plastic wrap and microwave 4 minutes; rotate dish 1/2 turn. Microwave until fish flakes easily with fork, 3 to 5 minutes longer. Sprinkle with almonds and cheese; cover and let stand 3 minutes.

Hot Pepper Snapper

5 SERVINGS; 205 CALORIES PER SERVING

1 can (16 ounces) whole tomatoes
1 medium onion, chopped
2 large cloves garlic
1 or 2 canned jalapeño peppers
1/4 cup sunflower seeds
1/4 teaspoon ground cumin
1 pound red snapper fillets
1/4 teaspoon salt
1 cup coarsely crushed corn chips

Place half of the tomatoes, onion, garlic, peppers, sunflower seeds and cumin in blender container. Cover and blend on high speed until smooth, about 10 seconds. Repeat with remaining half of ingredients.

If fish fillets are large, cut into 5 serving pieces. Arrange fish with thickest parts to outside edges in ungreased microwavable dish, 8 × 8 × 2 inches; sprinkle with salt. Pour tomato mixture over fish. Cover tightly and microwave on high 5 minutes. Sprinkle with corn chips; rotate dish 1/2 turn. Microwave uncovered until fish flakes easily with fork, 2 to 3 minutes longer. Let stand 3 minutes.

Cod with Hot Salsa

Hot Salsa (below)
1 pound cod or lean fish fillets
1 tablespoon reduced-calorie margarine,
    melted
1 tablespoon finely snipped fresh cilan-
    tro or 1 teaspoon dried cilantro leaves,
    if desired
1/4 teaspoon salt
1 clove garlic, crushed

Prepare Hot Salsa. If fish fillets are large, cut into 4 serving pieces. Arrange fish, thickest parts to outside edges, in square microwavable dish, 8 × 8 × 2 inches. Mix margarine, cilantro, salt and garlic; brush over fish. Cover with vented plastic wrap and microwave on high 3 minutes; rotate dish 1/2 turn. Microwave until fish flakes easily with fork, 3 to 5 minutes longer. Let stand covered 3 minutes. Serve with Hot Salsa; garnish with lime wedges, if desired.

HOT SALSA

1/2 cup chopped onion (about 1 medium)
1 tablespoon finely snipped fresh cilan-
    tro or 1 teaspoon dried cilantro leaves,
    if desired
1 tablespoon lemon juice
1 teaspoon vegetable oil
1 1/2 teaspoons snipped fresh oregano
    leaves or 1/2 teaspoon dried oregano
    leaves
3 cloves garlic, crushed
1 1/2 cups finely chopped tomatoes (about
    2 medium)
1 canned jalapeño pepper, seeded and
    finely chopped

Mix all ingredients for Hot Salsa in 4-cup microwavable measure. Cover with vented plastic wrap and microwave on high 2 minutes; stir. Microwave until hot and bubbly, 2 to 3 minutes longer. Drain, if desired. Serve with fish; garnish with lime wedges, if desired.

Garlic Cod

1 pound cod fillets
1/4 teaspoon salt
Dash of pepper
2 tablespoons margarine or butter, melted
1 tablespoon lemon juice
1/2 teaspoon onion powder
1/4 teaspoon paprika
5 large cloves garlic, finely chopped
2 tablespoons margarine or butter
1 tablespoon olive or vegetable oil
5 lemon wedges

If fish fillets are large, cut into 5 serving pieces. Sprinkle both sides with salt and pepper. Mix melted margarine, the lemon juice, onion powder and paprika. Dip fish into margarine mixture. Arrange fish, with thickest parts to outside edges, in ungreased microwavable dish, 8 × 8 × 2 inches. Pour remaining margarine mixture over fish. Cover tightly and microwave on high 2 minutes; rotate dish 1/2 turn. Microwave until fish flakes easily with fork, 2 to 4 minutes longer. Let stand 3 minutes. Place garlic, 2 tablespoons margarine and the oil in 2-cup microwavable measure. Cover loosely and microwave until garlic is brown, 4 to 5 minutes; pour over fish. Serve with lemon wedges.

Smoky Catfish

1 pound catfish or lean fish fillets
2 tablespoons lemon juice
1 tablespoon soy sauce
1 1/2 teaspoons liquid smoke
1 clove garlic, finely chopped
1 tablespoon snipped fresh chives

If fish fillets are large, cut into 4 serving pieces. Arrange fish fillets, thickest parts to outside edges, in microwavable dish, 12 × 7 1/2 × 2 inches. Mix remaining ingredients except chives; brush over fish. Cover and refrigerate about 30 minutes, brushing twice. Cover tightly and microwave on high 3 minutes; rotate dish 1/2 turn. Microwave until fish flakes easily with fork, 3 to 5 minutes longer. Sprinkle with chives.

Following pages: Cod with Hot Salsa

Fish Fillets with Sour Cream

4 SERVINGS; 280 CALORIES PER SERVING

1 pound fish fillets
4 ounces mushrooms, sliced
1 small onion, chopped
1 tablespoon margarine or butter
1/2 teaspoon salt
1/8 teaspoon pepper
1/2 cup dairy sour cream
3 tablespoons grated Parmesan cheese
2 tablespoons dry bread crumbs
Paprika
Snipped parsley

If fish fillets are large, cut into 4 serving pieces. Pat fish dry with paper towels. Arrange fish, with thickest parts to outside edges, in rectangular microwavable dish, 12 × 7½ × 2 inches or 10 × 6 × 1½ inches. Place mushrooms, onion and margarine in 4-cup microwavable measure. Cover tightly and microwave on high until onion is crisp-tender, 2 to 4 minutes; stir. Spoon mushroom mixture over fish; sprinkle with salt and pepper. Cover with waxed paper and microwave on high 3 minutes; spoon off liquid. Mix sour cream and cheese; spread over mushroom mixture. Sprinkle with bread crumbs. Microwave uncovered until fish flakes easily with fork, 3 to 5 minutes. Sprinkle with paprika and parsley.

Parmesan Fish Fillets

3 SERVINGS; 300 CALORIES PER SERVING

3 fish fillets (about 1 pound)
1/2 teaspoon salt
1/8 teaspoon pepper
1/2 cup dairy sour cream
2 tablespoons grated Parmesan cheese
1/4 teaspoon paprika
1/4 teaspoon snipped fresh tarragon leaves
   or 1/8 teaspoon dried tarragon leaves
3 green onions (with tops), sliced (about
   3 tablespoons)

Roll up fish fillets; place seam sides down in square microwavable dish, 8 × 8 × 2 inches. Sprinkle with salt and pepper. Cover with waxed paper and microwave on high 3 minutes; drain. Mix sour cream, cheese, paprika and tarragon; spread over fish. Cover loosely and microwave until fish flakes easily with fork, 3 to 6 minutes. Sprinkle with onions. Let stand covered 2 minutes.

Pike with Mustard Cream Sauce

4 SERVINGS; 130 CALORIES PER SERVING

1 pound pike or lean fish fillets
2 tablespoons reduced-calorie sour cream
2 tablespoons coarse-grained mustard
2 tablespoons reduced-calorie Italian
    dressing
½ cup chopped onion (about 1 medium)

Arrange fish with thickest parts to outside edges in microwavable dish, 12 × 7½ × 2 inches. Cover with waxed paper and microwave on high 3 minutes; rotate dish ½ turn. Microwave until fish flakes easily with fork, 3 to 5 minutes longer. Let stand covered 3 minutes.

Mix remaining ingredients. Serve with fish.

Orange Roughy with Tarragon Sauce

4 SERVINGS; 125 CALORIES PER SERVING

1 pound orange roughy or lean fish
    fillets
¼ teaspoon salt
1 tablespoon lemon juice
½ teaspoon snipped fresh tarragon leaves
    or ⅛ teaspoon dried tarragon leaves
Paprika
Tarragon Sauce (below)

If fish fillets are large, cut into 4 serving pieces. Arrange fish, thickest parts to outside edges, in square microwavable dish, 8 × 8 × 2 inches; sprinkle with salt. Drizzle with lemon juice; sprinkle with tarragon and paprika. Cover tightly and microwave on high 3 minutes; rotate dish ½ turn. Microwave until fish flakes easily with fork, 3 to 5 minutes longer. Serve with Tarragon Sauce.

TARRAGON SAUCE

⅓ cup nonfat plain yogurt
1 tablespoon reduced-calorie mayonnaise
    or salad dressing
½ teaspoon snipped fresh tarragon leaves
    or ⅛ teaspoon dried tarragon leaves
Dash salt

Mix all ingredients for Tarragon Sauce in 1-cup microwavable measure. Microwave uncovered on high, stirring every 15 seconds, about 45 seconds.

Following pages: Orange Roughy with Tarragon Sauce

Poached Fish
with Dijon-Dill Sauce

4 SERVINGS; 140 CALORIES PER SERVING

1 pound cod or firm lean fish fillets
1 cup hot water
⅓ cup skim milk
½ teaspoon salt
1 lemon, pared, thinly sliced and seeded
Dijon-Dill Sauce (below)

If fish fillets are large, cut into 4 serving pieces. Mix 1 cup hot water, the milk, salt and lemon slices in square microwavable dish, 8 × 8 × 2 inches. Cover with vented plastic wrap and microwave on high to boiling. Add fish with thickest parts to outside edges. Cover with with vented plastic wrap and microwave until fish flakes easily with fork, 5 to 7 minutes. Carefully remove fish with slotted spatula. Serve fish with Dijon-Dill Sauce.

DIJON-DILL SAUCE

⅔ cup skim milk
1 tablespoon Dijon-style mustard
2 teaspoons cornstarch
1½ teaspoons snipped fresh dill or
  ½ teaspoon dried dill weed
⅛ teaspoon salt

Mix all ingredients for Dijon-Dill Sauce in 2-cup microwavable measure. Microwave uncovered on high, stirring every minute, until thickened, 2 to 3 minutes.

· 5 ·

FISH AND VEGETABLES

Salmon Steaks with Asparagus and Peas

4 SERVINGS; 200 CALORIES PER SERVING

4 small salmon or halibut steaks, each
    about 1 inch thick (about 1½ pounds)
½ teaspoon salt
1½ teaspoons snipped rosemary leaves or
    ½ teaspoon dried rosemary leaves,
    crushed
1 tablespoon lemon juice
½ pound asparagus, cut into 2-inch
    pieces
1 cup fresh or frozen green peas
Lemon wedges

Arrange fish steaks in square microwavable dish, 8 × 8 × 2 inches. Sprinkle with salt, rosemary and lemon juice. Arrange asparagus and peas on fish. Cover with vented plastic wrap and microwave on high 5 minutes; rotate dish ½ turn. Microwave until fish flakes easily with fork and vegetables are crisp-tender, 4 to 5 minutes. Serve with lemon wedges.

Herbed Fish Steaks

2 medium carrots, coarsely shredded
1 medium leek, cut into thin strips
1 medium zucchini, cut into thin strips
1 medium stalk celery, cut into thin strips
3 fish steaks, each 1 inch thick (about 2 pounds)
2 tablespoons margarine or butter, melted
1½ teaspoons snipped fresh marjoram leaves or ½ teaspoon dried marjoram leaves
1½ teaspoons snipped fresh rosemary leaves or ½ teaspoon dried rosemary leaves, crushed
1 teaspoon salt
6 thin lemon slices

Mix vegetables and arrange in ungreased rectangular microwavable dish, 12 × 7½ × 2 inches. Cut each fish steak into halves; arrange on vegetables. Drizzle with margarine; sprinkle with herbs and salt. Place lemon slice on each piece fish. Cover with vented plastic wrap and microwave on high 5 minutes; rotate dish ½ turn. Microwave until fish flakes easily with fork, 6 to 8 minutes longer.

Orange Roughy with Red Peppers

1 pound orange roughy or lean fish fillets
1 small onion, cut into thin slices
2 red or green bell peppers, cut into julienne strips
1 tablespoon snipped fresh thyme leaves or 1 teaspoon dried thyme leaves
¼ teaspoon pepper

If fish fillets are large, cut into 4 serving pieces. Layer onion and bell peppers in rectangular microwavable dish, 12 × 7½ × 2 inches; sprinkle with half the thyme and half of the pepper. Cover with vented plastic wrap and microwave on high 2 minutes. Arrange fish, thickest parts to outside edges, on bell peppers; sprinkle with remaining thyme and pepper. Cover and microwave 4 minutes; rotate dish ½ turn. Microwave until fish flakes easily with fork, 3 to 5 minutes longer. Let stand covered 3 minutes.

Oriental Fish Fillets

4 SERVINGS; 150 CALORIES PER SERVING

1 pound fish fillets
3 tablespoons soy sauce
1/4 teaspoon ground ginger
1 clove garlic, finely chopped
2 medium green peppers, cut into 1-inch
   pieces
8 ounces mushrooms, cut into halves

Cut fish fillets into 4 serving pieces. Mix soy sauce, ginger and garlic; brush on both sides of fish. Arrange fish, with thickest parts to outside edges, in square microwavable dish, 8 × 8 × 2 inches. Top with vegetables. Cover with vented plastic wrap and microwave on high 4 minutes; rotate dish 1/2 turn. Microwave until fish flakes easily with fork and vegetables are crisp-tender, 4 to 5 minutes longer.

Fish Steaks on Steamed Vegetables

4 SERVINGS; 225 CALORIES PER SERVING

4 small fish steaks, each about 1 inch
   thick (about 1 1/2 pounds)
1 tablespoon snipped fresh savory leaves
   or 1 teaspoon dried savory leaves
Salt and pepper to taste
4 thin slices lemon
1 tablespoon margarine or butter
1 medium onion, sliced and separated
   into rings
1 small yellow pepper, cut into 1/4-inch
   slices
1 small red pepper, cut into 1/4-inch slices
8 ounces fresh spinach, coarsely chopped
   (about 6 cups)

Arrange fish steaks, with thickest parts to outside edges, in square microwavable dish, 8 × 8 × 2 inches. Sprinkle with savory, salt and pepper; place lemon slice on each fish steak. Cover with vented plastic wrap and microwave on high 4 minutes; rotate dish 1/2 turn. Microwave until fish flakes easily with fork, 4 to 5 minutes longer. Let stand covered.

Place margarine, onion and yellow and red peppers in 1 1/2-quart microwavable casserole. Cover tightly and microwave on high until vegetables are crisp-tender, 3 to 4 minutes; stir in spinach. Cover tightly and microwave just until spinach is hot, 1 to 2 minutes. Serve fish over vegetables.

Following pages: Fish Steaks on Steamed Vegetables

Baked Fish, Spanish Style

6 SERVINGS; 210 CALORIES PER SERVING

1½ pounds fish steaks or fillets, cut into
   serving pieces
1 teaspoon salt
¼ teaspoon paprika
¼ teaspoon pepper
1 green pepper, cut into rings
1 small onion, sliced
2 tablespoons lemon juice
2 tablespoons olive or vegetable oil
1 clove garlic, finely chopped
1 tomato, sliced
Lemon wedges

Arrange fish, with thickest parts to outside edges, in square microwavable dish, 8 × 8 × 2 inches. Sprinkle with salt, paprika and pepper. Top with green pepper rings and onion slices. Mix lemon juice, oil and garlic; pour over fish. Cover tightly and microwave on high 4 minutes. Top with tomato slices. Rotate dish ½ turn. Cover tightly and microwave until fish flakes easily with fork, 4 to 6 minutes. Let stand covered 3 minutes. Garnish with lemon wedges.

Steamed Grouper with Spinach

4 SERVINGS; 175 CALORIES PER SERVING

1 pound grouper or lean fish fillets
6 cloves garlic, thinly sliced
1 small onion, sliced
2 teaspoons olive or vegetable oil
½ teaspoon paprika
¼ teaspoon salt
¼ teaspoon pepper
⅓ cup dry white wine
2 packages (10 ounces each) frozen
   spinach, cooked and drained
½ lemon, cut into 4 wedges

If fish fillets are large, cut into 4 serving pieces. Mix garlic, onion and oil in square microwavable dish, 8 × 8 × 2 inches. Cover tightly and microwave until onion is softened, 1 to 2 minutes. Arrange fish, thickest parts to outside edges, on onion; sprinkle with paprika, salt and pepper. Pour wine around fish. Cover and microwave 4 minutes; rotate dish ½ turn. Microwave until fish flakes easily with fork, 3 to 5 minutes longer.

Arrange cooked spinach on deep platter. Carefully remove fish, garlic and onion with slotted spoon; place on spinach. Serve with lemon wedges.

Vegetable-stuffed Sole

6 SERVINGS; 180 CALORIES PER SERVING

24 carrot strips, each about 3 × ¼ inch
  (about 2 medium carrots)
1 tablespoon dry white wine
1½ teaspoons salt
1½ teaspoons snipped dill or ½ teaspoon
  dried dill weed
¼ teaspoon pepper
6 sole fillets (about 2 pounds)
18 green pepper strips, each about 3 × ¼
  inch (about 1 medium green pepper)
3 tablespoons dry white wine
2 tablespoons margarine or butter
2 tablespoons all-purpose flour
½ teaspoon salt
⅛ teaspoon pepper
1 cup milk
¼ cup dry white wine

Place carrot strips in rectangular microwavable dish, 11 × 7 × 1½ inches; add 1 tablespoon wine. Cover tightly and microwave on high until crisp-tender, about 4 minutes. Remove with slotted spoon. Mix 1½ teaspoons salt, the dill and ¼ teaspoon pepper; sprinkle over sole fillets.

Divide carrot and green pepper strips among fillets. Roll up; arrange seam sides down around sides of dish. Drizzle with 3 table-spoons wine. Cover tightly and microwave on high 5 minutes; rotate dish ½ turn. Micro-wave until fish flakes very easily with fork, 5 to 7 minutes longer. Let stand covered 3 min-utes. Arrange fish on warm platter; keep warm.

Microwave margarine in 4-cup microwavable measure uncovered on high until melted, 15 to 30 seconds; stir in flour, ½ teaspoon salt and ⅛ teaspoon pepper. Gradually stir in milk and ¼ cup wine. Microwave uncovered on high stirring every minute, until thickened, about 4 minutes.

Pour sauce over fish. Garnish with fresh snipped dill, if desired.

Fish with Vegetables

1 pound fish fillets
½ teaspoon salt
⅛ teaspoon pepper
2 tablespoons margarine or butter, melted
1 tablespoon lemon juice
1 medium zucchini, cut into ¼-inch slices
1 small green pepper, cut into ¼-inch strips
1 small red onion, sliced

If fish fillets are large, cut into 4 serving pieces. Place fish in rectangular microwavable dish, 10 × 6 × 1½ inches; sprinkle with salt and pepper. Mix 2 tablespoons melted margarine and the lemon juice; pour over fish. Top with zucchini, green pepper and onion. Cover tightly and microwave on high until fish flakes easily with fork and vegetables are tender, 8 to 11 minutes.

Fish Baked in Lettuce Packets

6 large lettuce leaves
1 medium carrot, shredded
1 small zucchini, shredded
1½ pounds fish fillets, cut into 6 serving pieces
1 tablespoon snipped fresh marjoram leaves or 1 teaspoon dried marjoram leaves
Salt and pepper to taste
Margarine or butter

Place a few lettuce leaves at a time in hot water. Let stand until wilted, 1 to 2 minutes; drain. Mound a portion of carrot and zucchini near stem end of each lettuce leaf. Place 1 piece of fish on vegetables. Sprinkle with marjoram, salt and pepper; dot with margarine. Fold lettuce leaf over fish. Repeat with remaining lettuce leaves.

Place rolls seam sides down in rectangular microwavable dish, 12 × 7½ × 2 inches. Cover with vented plastic wrap and microwave on high 4 minutes; rotate dish ½ turn. Microwave until fish flakes easily with fork, 5 to 6 minutes longer.

Cod Continental

4 SERVINGS; 145 CALORIES PER SERVING

6 to 8 large romaine leaves
1-pound cod fillet, about 1 inch thick
½ teaspoon salt
2 cloves garlic, crushed
2 green onions
¼ cup thinly sliced radishes
2 tablespoons lemon juice
1 tablespoon olive or vegetable oil
Lemon wedges

Pour boiling water over romaine leaves. Let stand until limp, about 2 minutes; drain. Arrange half of the leaves on microwave roasting rack in oblong baking dish, 12 × 7½ × 2 inches. Place fish on leaves. Rub salt and garlic on fish. Arrange onions and radishes on fish; pour lemon juice and oil over fish. Place remaining leaves on top of fish.

Cover loosely and microwave on high 5 minutes; turn dish ½ turn. Microwave until fish flakes easily with fork, 8 to 10 minutes, turning dish ½ turn every 4 minutes. Remove leaves. Serve fish with lemon wedges.

Fish with Summer Vegetables

4 SERVINGS; 175 CALORIES PER SERVING

1 pound pollack or lean fish fillets
1 tablespoon lemon juice
Freshly ground pepper
1 cup thinly sliced zucchini or yellow
  squash (about 1 medium)
1 small onion, thinly sliced
1 tablespoon snipped fresh basil leaves
  or 1 teaspoon dried basil leaves
1 can (8 ounces) stewed tomatoes,
  undrained
2 tablespoons grated Parmesan cheese

Arrange fish, thickest parts to outside edges, in rectangular microwavable dish, 11 × 7 × 1½ inches; sprinkle with lemon juice and pepper. Layer zucchini, onion, basil and tomatoes over fish. Cover tightly and microwave on high 5 minutes; rotate dish ½ turn. Microwave until fish flakes easily with fork, 3 to 6 minutes longer. Sprinkle with cheese.

Following pages: Fish Baked in Lettuce Packets

Fish with Green Vegetables

5 SERVINGS; 180 CALORIES PER SERVING

1 pound fish fillets
1 teaspoon salt
¼ teaspoon pepper
1 package (10 ounces) frozen peas
1 medium cucumber, cut lengthwise into fourths, then crosswise into 1-inch pieces
1 medium stalk celery, cut diagonally into ¼-inch slices
1 small onion, cut into ¼-inch slices
½ teaspoon salt
1 tablespoon lemon juice
2 tablespoons margarine or butter

If fillets are large, cut into 5 serving pieces. Place in 2-quart microwavable casserole. Sprinkle with 1 teaspoon salt and the pepper. Cover and microwave on high until fish is almost done, 3½ to 4 minutes.

Rinse frozen peas under running cold water to separate; drain. Spoon peas, cucumber, celery and onion onto fish; sprinkle with ½ teaspoon salt and the lemon juice. Dot with margarine. Cover and microwave until vegetables are crisp-tender and fish flakes easily with fork, about 6 minutes. Sprinkle with paprika and garnish with lemon wedges, if desired.

Fish with Crunchy Vegetables

5 SERVINGS; 180 CALORIES PER SERVING

1 pound fish fillets
½ teaspoon salt
⅛ teaspoon pepper
⅛ teaspoon paprika
1 medium carrot, shredded (about ½ cup)
1 large stalk celery, finely chopped (about ¾ cup)
3 green onions, finely chopped (about ⅓ cup)
½ teaspoon salt
1 tablespoon lemon juice
2 tablespoons margarine or butter

If fish fillets are large, cut into 5 serving pieces. Place fish in ungreased square microwavable dish, 8 × 8 × 2 inches. Sprinkle with ½ teaspoon salt, the pepper and paprika. Cover and microwave on high until fish is almost done, 3½ to 4 minutes. Spoon carrot, celery and onions onto fish; sprinkle with ½ teaspoon salt and the lemon juice. Dot with margarine. Cover and microwave until vegetables are crisp-tender and fish flakes easily with fork, 2 to 3 minutes.

Fish with Green Chilies

4 SERVINGS; 145 CALORIES PER SERVING

1 pound lean fish fillets
1 medium onion, thinly sliced
¼ teaspoon salt
¼ teaspoon coarsely ground pepper
1 can (4 ounces) chopped green chilies, drained
12 pimiento-stuffed olives
3 tablespoons dry white wine
1 tablespoon lemon juice
Lemon wedges

If fish fillets are large, cut into 4 serving pieces. Arrange onion in square microwavable dish 8 × 8 × 2 inches; place fish on onion with thickest parts to outside edges of dish. Sprinkle with salt and pepper. Spoon chilies over fish; top with olives. Mix wine and lemon juice; pour over fish. Cover with vented plastic wrap and microwave on high 4 minutes; rotate dish ½ turn. Microwave until fish flakes easily with fork, 3 to 5 minutes longer. Let stand covered 3 minutes. Serve with lemon wedges.

Creole Catfish

6 SERVINGS; 265 CALORIES PER SERVING

2 pounds catfish, red snapper, cod or haddock fillets
1 can (28 ounces) whole tomatoes, drained
⅓ cup chopped green pepper
2 tablespoons snipped parsley
1 tablespoon lemon juice
½ teaspoon salt
½ teaspoon ground red pepper
1 medium onion, chopped
1 clove garlic, crushed
3 cups hot cooked rice

Arrange fillets, thickest parts to outside edges, in rectangular microwavable dish, 11 × 7 × 1½ inches. Mix tomatoes and remaining ingredients except rice; break up tomatoes. Pour over fish. Cover tightly and microwave on high 6 minutes; rotate dish ½ turn. Microwave until fish flakes very easily with fork, 4 to 5 minutes longer. Let stand covered 3 minutes. Serve over rice. Garnish fish with lemon slices sprinkled with snipped parsley, if desired.

Cod with Marinated Tomatoes

5 SERVINGS; 125 CALORIES PER SERVING

2 medium tomatoes, chopped (about
  1½ cups)
¼ cup sliced green onions (with tops)
2 tablespoons vinegar
2 tablespoons water
1 tablespoon capers
½ teaspoon salt
¼ teaspoon red pepper sauce
1 pound cod fillets

Mix tomatoes, onions, vinegar, water, capers, salt and the pepper sauce in glass jar or bowl. Cover and let stand at room temperature at least 4 hours.

If fish fillets are large, cut into 5 serving pieces. Arrange fish with thickest parts to outside edges in microwavable dish, 8 × 8 × 2 inches. Cover tightly and microwave on high 3 minutes; rotate dish ½ turn. Microwave until fish flakes easily with fork, 2 to 4 minutes longer. Remove fish with slotted spoon. Drain tomato mixture; spoon over fish.

Mediterranean Halibut

4 SERVINGS; 140 CALORIES PER SERVING

1 pound halibut or lean fish fillets
2 tablespoons lemon juice
1 tablespoon chopped onion
1 tablespoon chopped pimiento
1 tablespoon coarsely chopped pimiento-
  stuffed olives
1 tablespoon capers
1 tablespoon olive or vegetable oil

If fish fillets are large, cut into 4 serving pieces. Arrange fish, thickest parts to outside edges, in square microwavable dish, 8 × 8 × 2 inches. Mix remaining ingredients; spread over fish. Cover and refrigerate at least 30 minutes, but no longer than 6 hours. Cover tightly and microwave on high 3 minutes; rotate dish ½ turn. Microwave until fish flakes easily with fork, 3 to 5 minutes longer. Let stand covered 3 minutes.

Southern Tuna Casserole

2 cans (6½ ounces each) tuna in water,
    drained
1 can (20 ounces) hominy, drained
1 can (8 ounces) tomato sauce
1 cup chopped green bell pepper (about
    1 medium)
¼ cup chopped onion (about 1 small)
½ teaspoon ground cumin
½ cup shredded Cheddar cheese
    (2 ounces)

Mix all ingredients except cheese in 1½-quart microwavable casserole. Cover tightly and microwave on high 3 minutes; stir. Cover tightly and microwave until hot, 4 to 6 minutes longer; sprinkle with cheese. Let stand covered until cheese melts, about 3 minutes.

Curried Tuna

¼ cup margarine or butter
2 teaspoons curry powder
2 green onions (with tops), thinly sliced
3 cups cooked regular rice
½ teaspoon salt
¼ teaspoon ground ginger
⅛ teaspoon garlic powder
⅛ teaspoon ground red pepper
1 can (12½ ounces) tuna in water,
    drained
1 hard-cooked egg, chopped
1 tablespoon snipped parsley

Place margarine, curry powder and onions in 2-quart microwavable casserole. Cover tightly and microwave on high until margarine is melted, 1 to 2 minutes. Stir rice, salt, ginger, garlic powder, red pepper and tuna into casserole. Cover tightly and microwave until tuna is hot, 3 to 5 minutes. Sprinkle with egg and parsley. Serve with chutney, if desired.

Following pages: Mediterranean Halibut

Salmon with Artichokes

8 SERVINGS; 215 CALORIES PER SERVING

4 slices bacon, cut into ½-inch pieces
1 medium onion, sliced
1 medium stalk celery, diagonally sliced
1 package (10 ounces) frozen artichoke
    hearts
1 package (10 ounces) frozen green peas
2 tablespoons water
½ teaspoon salt
¾ teaspoon snipped fresh tarragon leaves
    or ¼ teaspoon dried tarragon leaves
¼ teaspoon pepper
1 can (15½ ounces) salmon, drained and
    flaked
1 jar (2 ounces) diced pimiento, drained
1 tablespoon lemon juice
3 cups hot cooked spaghetti

Place bacon in 2-quart microwavable casserole. Cover with paper towel and microwave on high stirring every 2 minutes until crisp, 3 to 4 minutes. Remove with slotted spoon and drain on paper towel; reserve.

Stir onion and celery into bacon fat. Microwave uncovered, stirring every minute, until onion is tender, 2 to 3 minutes. Stir in artichokes, peas, 2 tablespoons water, the salt, tarragon and pepper. Cover tightly and microwave 5 minutes; stir. Cover and microwave until vegetables are almost tender, 3 to 5 minutes. Stir in salmon, pimiento and lemon juice. Cover and microwave until salmon is hot, 2 to 3 minutes longer. Toss with spaghetti; sprinkle with reserved bacon.

RED SPOON TIPS

Microwave Equipment Safety Checklist

- Use oven-tempered glassware, microwavable china, ceramic plates, casseroles, paper and plastic (most dishwasher-safe plastics are also microwavable).
- Test whether utensils are microwavable. Place the utensil in the microwave oven alongside 1 cup cool water in a glass measure. Microwave uncovered on high 1 minute. If the water is warm but the utensil remains cool, then it is most likely microwavable. If the utensil is warm, do not use it for microwave cooking.
- Microwavable, undecorated paper towels are excellent for absorbing grease or preventing splatter, as with cooking bacon. Use only microwavable paper toweling; it is free of the tiny metal fragments that may be found in recycled paper toweling, and it has been formulated specifically for direct contact with food.
- When microwaving commercially packaged foods in plastic cooking pouches, follow the directions on the package.

- Using metal in the microwave oven is acceptable only when the metal is specifically designed for microwave cooking. Examples include metal microwave shelves and such microwavable cookware as browning dishes, pizza crispers and egg poachers. Use of dishes with metallic trim, casseroles with metal parts, and metal twist ties can cause "arcing." Arcing produces blue-white sparks (and sharp crackling sounds) and can damage cookware or the oven interior.
- Bread boards and unlacquered wicker baskets can be placed briefly in the microwave oven to warm foods. Be sure they have no metal parts (nails, staples or fasteners).

Micro-Hints

ALMONDS: To blanch, place ½ cup water in small microwavable bowl. Microwave uncovered on high until boiling, 1½ to 2½ minutes. Add ¼ cup whole natural almonds. Microwave uncovered until skin is soft, 30 to 45 seconds. Drain hot water from bowl; cover almonds with cold water. Skin.

To toast, place 2 tablespoons sliced almonds and 1 teaspoon margarine or butter in 6-ounce custard cup. Microwave uncovered on high, stirring every 30 seconds, until almonds are light brown, 3 to 4 minutes.

BREAD CRUMBS: Toss ½ cup soft breadcrumbs (about 1 slice bread) and ½ teaspoon margarine or butter, melted, in microwavable pie plate. Microwave uncovered on high, stirring every 30 seconds, until dried, about 1 minute.

COCONUT: To toast, place ¼ cup flaked coconut in microwavable pie plate. Microwave uncovered on high, stirring every 30 seconds, until golden brown, 30 to 45 seconds.

CROUTONS: Arrange ½ cup ½-inch bread cubes in microwavable pie plate. Microwave uncovered on high 1 minute; stir. Microwave uncovered until dry, 30 to 60 seconds longer.

EGGS: Never microwave an egg in the shell; it can explode. When poaching or steaming raw eggs out of the shell, prick the yolk several times with a wooden pick. Eggs become rubbery when overcooked, so note doneness tests and standing times.

FISH AND SEAFOOD: Arrange with thickest pieces to the outside of the dish. For fish with a crispy coating, cook uncovered on a microwave rack. Canned fish and seafood—tuna, salmon, clams, shrimp and so forth—are already cooked; microwave just until heated through.

FRUIT: You'll get more juice from citrus fruits if you warm them before squeezing. Microwave 1 lemon, lime or orange on medium-low (30%) until warm, 20 to 30 seconds.

GROUND BEEF: You can cook and drain crumbled ground beef at the same time. Place the beef in a microwavable colander and set the colander in a microwavable casserole. Cover loosely and cook as directed.

LIQUOR: To warm liquor for flaming foods, place 2 tablespoons liquor in 1-cup microwavable measure. Microwave uncovered on high until warm, 15 to 20 seconds. Pour into metal ladle or serving spoon; ignite and pour.

OYSTERS: Arrange scrubbed oysters on a microwavable plate with hinges toward the rim of the plate. Cover tightly and microwave on high until shells open slightly, 1 to 1½ minutes. (Remove oysters as they begin to open.) Oyster meat will be slightly cooked.

PORK: When checking the internal temperature for doneness, check in more than one place for a reading of 170°F. Do not substitute uncooked pork for fully-cooked pork (ham, Polish sausage and luncheon meats), because the cooking times and methods vary.

VEGETABLES AND FRUITS: Vegetable skins will split or burst if they are not pierced or partially pared before microwave cooking. Potatoes and apples, for example, will split their skins, while whole squashes can burst.

Microwave Power Settings

While some foods microwave well at the high setting, others are best microwaved at lower settings. If your microwave oven doesn't have the same settings as those below, refer to the manufacturer's manual to determine the percent of power to which your settings correspond. Always use the first power setting given in the directions unless a change is indicated.

POWER LEVEL SETTING	PERCENT OF HIGH SETTING
High	100%
Medium-high	70%
Medium	50%
Medium-low	30%
Low	10%

MICROWAVING FRESH VEGETABLES

Artichokes (French—Globe)

FOR 4 SERVINGS: USE 4 (1 PER SERVING)

Prepare: Remove any discolored leaves and all the small leaves at the base of the artichoke; trim stem even with artichoke base. Cutting straight across, slice 1 inch off top; discard top. Snip off points of the remaining leaves with scissors. Rinse artichoke under cold water.

Cook: Place 1 cup water, 1 teaspoon cooking oil, 1 teaspoon lemon juice, 1 small clove garlic (cut into fourths), ⅛ teaspoon salt and artichokes in 3-quart casserole. Cover tightly and microwave on high 7 minutes; rotate casserole ½ turn. Microwave until leaves pull out easily and bottom is tender when pierced with a knife, 7 to 9 minutes longer. Carefully remove artichokes; place upside down to drain.

Artichokes (Jerusalem)

FOR 4 SERVINGS: USE 1½ POUNDS

Prepare: Scrub artichokes; cut crosswise into ¼-inch slices.

Cook: Place ¼ cup water, ¼ teaspoon salt and artichokes in 1½-quart casserole. Cover tightly and microwave on high 5 minutes; stir. Cover and microwave until crisp-tender, 4 to 6 minutes longer; stir. Let stand 5 minutes; drain.

Asparagus

FOR 4 SERVINGS: USE 1½ POUNDS

Prepare: Break off tough ends as far down as stalks snap easily. Wash asparagus. Cut stalks into 1½-inch pieces or leave whole.

Cook: For asparagus cuts, place in 1½-quart casserole; add ¼ cup water. For spears, arrange lengthwise (tips in center) in baking dish, 10 × 6 × 1½ inches; add ¼ cup water. Cover tightly and microwave on high 3 minutes; stir cuts or rotate baking dish containing spears ½ turn. Cover and microwave until crisp-tender, 2 to 3 minutes longer. Let stand 1 minute; drain.

Beans (Green Lima)

FOR 4 SERVINGS: USE 3 POUNDS (UNSHELLED)

Prepare: Wash and shell lima beans just before cooking. To shell beans, remove thin outer edge of pod with sharp knife or scissors. Beans will slip out.

Cook: Place ¼ cup water and lima beans in 1½-quart casserole. Cover tightly and microwave on high 7 minutes; stir. Cover and microwave until tender, 7 to 9 minutes longer. Let stand 5 minutes; drain.

Beans (Green and Wax)

FOR 4 SERVINGS: USE 1 POUND

Prepare: Wash beans and remove ends. Cut into 1-inch pieces.

Cook: Place ½ cup water, ¼ teaspoon salt and beans in 1½-quart casserole. Cover tightly and microwave on high 5 minutes; stir. Cover and microwave until tender, 4 to 9 minutes longer. Let stand 5 minutes; drain.

Broccoli

FOR 6 SERVINGS: USE 1½ POUNDS

Prepare: Trim off large leaves. Remove tough ends of lower stems; wash broccoli.

Cook: For spears, cut broccoli lengthwise into thin stalks. If stems are thicker than 1 inch, make lengthwise gashes in each stem. Place ¼ cup water and ½ teaspoon salt in baking dish, 12 × 7½ × 2 inches, or 10-inch pie plate. Arrange broccoli with tips in center. Cover tightly and microwave on high 4 minutes; rotate baking dish or pie plate ½ turn. Microwave until tender, 3 to 5 minutes longer; drain.

Brussels Sprouts

FOR 4 SERVINGS: USE 1 POUND

Prepare: Remove any discolored leaves. Cut off stem ends; wash sprouts.

Cook: Place ¼ cup water and Brussels sprouts in 1½-quart casserole. Cover tightly and microwave on high 5 minutes; stir. Cover and microwave until tender when pierced with fork, 3 to 8 minutes longer. Let stand 5 minutes; drain.

Cabbage (Chinese, Celery)

FOR 4 OR 6 SERVINGS:
USE ABOUT 1 POUND (1 MEDIUM HEAD)

Prepare: Remove root ends. Wash cabbage; shred.

Cook: Place ¼ cup water, ¼ teaspoon salt and cabbage in 1½-quart casserole. Cover tightly and microwave on high 2 minutes; stir. Cover and microwave until crisp-tender, 2 to 4 minutes longer. Let stand 1 minute; drain.

Cabbage (Green Savoy, Red)

FOR 4 SERVINGS:
USE ¾ TO 1 POUND (1 SMALL HEAD)

Prepare: Remove outside leaves; wash cabbage. Shred cabbage and discard core. Or cut cabbage into 4 wedges and trim core to within ¼ inch of leaves.

Cook: For shredded, place ¼ cup water, ½ teaspoon salt and cabbage in 2-quart casserole. Cover tightly and microwave on high 4 minutes; stir. Cover and microwave until crisp-tender, 4 to 5 minutes longer. Let stand 3 minutes; drain.

For wedges, place ½ cup water and ½ teaspoon salt in 2-quart casserole. Arrange wedges spoke-fashion with core at outside edge of casserole. Cover tightly and microwave on high 5 minutes; rotate casserole ½ turn. Microwave until crisp-tender, 5 to 8 minutes longer. Let stand 5 minutes; drain.

Carrots

FOR 4 SERVINGS: USE 1 POUND

Prepare: Scrape carrots and remove ends. Cut carrots crosswise into ¼-inch slices.

Cook: Place ¼ cup water, ¼ teaspoon salt and carrots in 1-quart casserole. Cover tightly and microwave on high 4 minutes; stir. Cover and microwave until tender, 2 to 4 minutes longer; drain.

Cauliflower

FOR 4 SERVINGS: USE ABOUT 1 POUND (1 MEDIUM HEAD)

Prepare: Remove outer leaves and stalk. Cut off any discoloration; wash cauliflower. Leave whole and cut out cone-shaped center from core or separate into flowerets.

Cook: Place ¼ cup water and cauliflower in 1½-quart casserole. Cover tightly and microwave on high 4 minutes. Rotate casserole ¼ turn for whole cauliflower; stir flowerets. Cover and microwave until tender, 3 to 4 minutes longer; drain.

Celery (Pascal, Green, Golden, Bleached)

FOR 4 SERVINGS:
USE 1 MEDIUM BUNCH

Prepare: Remove leaves and trim off root ends. Remove any coarse strings; wash celery. Cut stalks into 1-inch pieces.

Cook: Place 2 tablespoons water, ¼ teaspoon salt and celery in 1½-quart casserole. Cover tightly and microwave on high 4 minutes; stir. Cover and microwave until tender, 3 to 5 minutes longer. Let stand 3 minutes; drain.

Celery Root (Celeriac)

FOR 4 SERVINGS: USE 1½ POUNDS

Prepare: Cut off any leaves or root fibers and pare thinly. Cut into ½-inch pieces.

Cook: Place ¼ cup water, ¼ teaspoon salt and celery root in 1½-quart casserole. Cover tightly and microwave on high 5 minutes; stir. Cover and microwave until crisp-tender, 4 to 6 minutes longer. Let stand 1 minute; drain.

Corn on the Cob

FOR 4 SERVINGS: USE 4 TO 8 EARS

Prepare: Refrigerate unhusked corn until ready to use. Husk 4 ears corn and remove silk just before cooking.

Cook: Wrap each ear of corn in waxed paper; twist ends. Arrange 2 inches apart in microwave. Microwave on high 5 minutes; turn corn over and rearrange ears. Microwave until tender, 4 to 6 minutes longer. Let stand 3 minutes.

Note: Corn can be microwaved in the husk, if desired. After microwaving, grasp silk and gently pull off before removing husks.

Eggplant

FOR 4 SERVINGS: USE 1½ POUNDS (1 MEDIUM)

Prepare: Just before cooking, wash eggplant and, if desired, pare. Cut into ½-inch cubes or ¼-inch slices.

Cook: For cubes, place 2 tablespoons water, ½ teaspoon salt and eggplant in 1½-quart casserole. Cover tightly and microwave on high until tender, stirring every 2 minutes, 6 to 8 minutes; drain.
For slices, place 2 tablespoons water and ½ teaspoon salt in 9-inch pie plate. Overlap eggplant slices in circle around edge of pie plate. Cover tightly and microwave on high 3 minutes; rotate pie plate ½ turn. Microwave until tender, 3 to 5 minutes longer; drain.

Greens (Spinach, Beet Tops, Chicory Escarole, Mustard Greens)

FOR 4 SERVINGS: USE 1 POUND

Prepare: Remove root ends and imperfect leaves. Wash greens several times, lifting out of the water each time; drain.

Cook: Place greens with just the water that clings to the leaves in 3-quart casserole or bowl. Cover tightly and microwave on high 3 minutes; stir. Cover and microwave until tender, 3 to 5 minutes longer. Let stand 3 minutes; drain.

Kohlrabi

FOR 3 OR 4 SERVINGS: USE 1½ POUNDS (6 TO 8 MEDIUM)

Prepare: Trim off root ends and vinelike stems. Wash and pare kohlrabi. Cut into ¼-inch slices.

Cook: Place ¼ cup water, ¼ teaspoon salt and kohlrabi in 1-quart casserole. Cover tightly and microwave on high 3 minutes; stir. Cover and microwave until tender, 3 to 5 minutes longer. Let stand covered 1 minute; drain.

Leeks

FOR 4 SERVINGS: USE 2 POUNDS (ABOUT 6 MEDIUM)

Prepare: Cut roots from leeks; remove woody green tops to within 2 inches of white part (save greens for soup or stew). Peel outside layer of bulbs. Cut large leeks lengthwise into fourths for pieces of similar size. Wash in cold water, spreading leaves to clean.

Cook: Place ¼ cup water, ½ teaspoon salt and leeks in 1½-quart casserole. Cover tightly and microwave on high 3 minutes; rotate casserole ½ turn. Microwave until tender, 3 to 5 minutes longer. Let stand 1 minute; drain.

Mushrooms

FOR 4 SERVINGS: USE 1 POUND

Prepare: Rinse mushrooms and trim off stem ends. Slice mushrooms parallel to stem in ¼-inch slices.

Cook: Place mushrooms in 1½-quart casserole. Cover tightly and microwave on high 2 minutes; stir. Cover and microwave until tender, 1 to 3 minutes longer. Let stand 1 minute; drain. Stir in 1 tablespoon margarine or butter.

Okra

FOR 4 SERVINGS: USE 1 POUND

Prepare: Remove tips; wash okra and cut into ½-inch slices.

Cook: Place ¼ cup water, ¼ teaspoon salt and okra in 1½-quart casserole. Cover tightly and microwave on high 3 minutes; stir. Cover and microwave until tender, 2 to 3 minutes longer. Let stand 1 minute.

Onions (Small White, Yellow, Red)

FOR 4 SERVINGS:
USE 1½ POUNDS (8 TO 10)

Prepare: Peel onions under running cold water (to prevent eyes from watering).

Cook: Place ¼ cup water, ¼ teaspoon salt and onions in 2-quart casserole. Cover tightly and microwave on high 3 minutes; stir. Cover and microwave until tender, 3 to 5 minutes longer. Let stand 3 minutes; drain.

Parsnips

FOR 4 SERVINGS: USE 1½ POUNDS (6 TO 8)

Prepare: Scrape or pare parsnips. Cut into ¼-inch slices.

Cook: Place ¼ cup water, ¼ teaspoon salt and parsnips in 1-quart casserole. Cover tightly and microwave on high 4 minutes; stir. Cover and microwave until tender, 4 to 6 minutes longer. Let stand 1 minute.

Chinese Pea Pods

FOR 3 SERVINGS: USE 1 POUND

Prepare: Wash pea pods; remove tips and strings.

Cook: Place ¼ cup water, ¼ teaspoon salt and pea pods in 1½-quart casserole. Cover tightly and microwave on high 3 minutes; stir. Cover and microwave until crisp-tender, 3 to 5 minutes longer. Let stand 3 minutes; drain.

Green Peas

FOR 4 SERVINGS: USE 3 POUNDS (UNSHELLED)

Prepare: Wash and shell peas just before cooking.

Cook: Place ¼ cup water and ½ teaspoon salt and peas in 1½-quart casserole. Cover tightly and microwave on high 4 minutes; stir. Cover and microwave until tender, 4 to 6 minutes longer. Let stand 3 minutes; drain.

Peppers (Green Bell)

FOR 4 SERVINGS:
USE 2 GREEN PEPPERS IF SLICED, 4 IF STUFFED

Prepare: Wash 2 green peppers; remove stems, seeds and membranes. Leave whole or cut into thin slices.

Cook: Place peppers in 1½-quart casserole. Cover tightly and microwave on high 2 minutes; stir. Cover and microwave until crisp-tender, 2 to 3 minutes longer. Let stand 1 minute.

Potatoes (Small New)

FOR 4 OR 5 SERVINGS: USE 1½ POUNDS (10 TO 14)

Prepare: Wash potatoes of similar size lightly and leave whole. Pierce potatoes to allow steam to escape, or pare narrow strip around centers.

Cook: Place ¼ cup water, ½ teaspoon salt and potatoes in 2-quart casserole, arranging larger potatoes at outside edge of casserole, small potatoes in center. Cover tightly and microwave on high 5 minutes; stir. Cover and microwave until tender, 5 to 10 minutes longer. Let stand 1 minute; drain.

Potatoes (White)

FOR 4 SERVINGS: USE 1½ POUNDS (4 MEDIUM)

Prepare. For whole potatoes, scrub oval potatoes (rather than long shapes) of similar size. Pierce potatoes to allow steam to escape. Or cut into 1-inch pieces.

Cook: For whole potatoes, arrange potatoes about 2 inches apart in circle in microwave. (If potatoes are long, old or dry, wrap each in waxed paper before placing in microwave. For crisper potato skins, sprinkle each dampened potato with salt.) Microwave potatoes uncovered on high until tender, 11 to 13 minutes. Let stand 5 minutes. (Potatoes hold their heat well; if microwaving a second vegetable, cook potatoes first.)

For cut-up potatoes, place ½ cup water, ½ teaspoon salt and potatoes in 2-quart casserole. Cover tightly and microwave on high 6 minutes; stir. Cover and microwave until tender, 5 to 7 minutes longer.

Potatoes (Sweet)

FOR 4 SERVINGS: USE 1½ POUNDS (ABOUT 4 MEDIUM)

Prepare: Wash sweet potatoes of similar size but do not pare. Pierce potatoes to allow steam to escape.

Cook: Arrange potatoes about 2 inches apart in circle on paper towel in microwave. Microwave uncovered on high until tender when pierced with fork, 8 to 15 minutes. Let stand 5 minutes.

Squash (Summer: Pattypan, Straightneck, Crookneck, Zucchini)

FOR 4 SERVINGS: USE 1½ POUNDS

Prepare: Wash squash; remove stem and blossom ends but do not pare. Cut into ½-inch slices or cubes.

Cook: Place ¼ cup water, ¼ teaspoon salt and squash in 1½-quart casserole. Cover tightly and microwave on high 4 minutes; stir. Cover and microwave until almost tender, 4 to 6 minutes longer (pattypan 5 to 9 minutes); stir. Cover squash and let stand 1 minute; drain.

Squash (Spaghetti)

FOR 6 SERVINGS:
USE ABOUT 2½ POUNDS (1 MEDIUM)

Prepare: Pierce squash in several places to allow steam to escape.

Cook: Place squash on paper towel in microwave. Microwave on high 8 minutes; turn squash over. Microwave until tender, 8 to 11 minutes longer; let stand 10 minutes. Cut in half crosswise; scoop out seeds. Unwind spaghetti-like flesh with fork and serve like pasta.

Squash (Winter: Acorn)

FOR 4 SERVINGS: USE ABOUT 2 POUNDS (2 MEDIUM)

Prepare: Pierce squash of similar size to allow steam to escape.

Cook: Place squash 2 inches apart in microwave. Microwave on high 4 to 6 minutes. Carefully cut into halves; remove seeds. Arrange squash halves with cut sides down in baking dish, 12 × 7½ × 2 inches. Cover tightly and microwave on high until tender, 5 to 8 minutes longer. Let stand 1 minute.

Tomatoes

FOR 4 SERVINGS: USE 2 POUNDS (ABOUT 6 MEDIUM)

Prepare: Wash tomatoes; cut into 8 wedges or ½-inch slices. Peel tomatoes before cutting, if desired.

Cook: Place tomatoes in 2-quart casserole. Cover tightly and microwave on high 4 minutes for wedges, 3 minutes for slices; gently stir. Cover and microwave until hot—wedges 3 to 4 minutes, slices 2 to 3 minutes. Let stand 1 minute.

Turnips (Yellow—Rutabagas)

FOR 4 SERVINGS:
USE 1½ POUNDS (1 LARGE OR 2 SMALL)

Prepare: Wash and pare thinly. Cut into ½-inch pieces.

Cook: Place ½ cup water, ½ teaspoon salt and rutabagas in 2-quart casserole. Cover tightly and microwave on high stirring every 5 minutes until tender, 14 to 17 minutes. Let stand 1 minute; drain.

Turnips (White)

FOR 4 SERVINGS: USE 1½ POUNDS (6 MEDIUM)

Prepare: If necessary, cut off tops. Wash and pare thinly; cut into ½-inch pieces.

Cook: Place ¼ cup water, ½ teaspoon salt and turnips in 2-quart casserole. Cover tightly and microwave on high, stirring every 4 minutes, until tender, 12 to 14 minutes. Let stand 1 minute; drain.

MICROWAVE TIME ON HIGH

VEGETABLE	1 SERVING (½ CUP)	2 SERVINGS (1 CUP)
Asparagus (cuts or spears)	1½ to 2 minutes	3½ to 4 minutes
Beans, green or wax (cuts)	2½ to 3 minutes	4 to 4½ minutes
Beans, lima	2 to 2½ minutes	3½ to 4½ minutes
Broccoli (cuts or spears)	2½ to 3 minutes	3½ to 4 minutes
Brussels sprouts	2½ to 3 minutes	4 to 5 minutes
Carrots (sliced)	2½ to 3 minutes	4 to 4½ minutes
Cauliflower (flowerets)	2 to 2½ minutes	3½ to 4 minutes
Corn, whole kernel	1¼ to 1½ minutes	2 to 2½ minutes
Corn on the cob	4 to 5 minutes (1 ear)	6 to 8 minutes (2 ears)
Mixed vegetables	1¼ to 1½ minutes	2½ to 3 minutes
Onions, small whole	1½ to 2 minutes	2½ to 3 minutes
Peas, green	1 to 1½ minutes	2½ to 3 minutes
Potatoes, white or sweet	conventional cooking recommended	

Canned Vegetables: Drain 8- to 9-ounce can of vegetables, reserving 1 tablespoon liquid for each ½ cup serving. Mix vegetables and liquid in casserole. Cover tightly and microwave on high 30 seconds to 1½ minutes for 1 serving, 1 to 2½ minutes for 2 servings.

Microwaving Frozen Vegetables for One or Two

Place frozen vegetables and 1 to 3 teaspoons water in 10-ounce or 21-ounce casserole. Cover tightly and microwave on high, stirring once, for amount of time directed in chart below. Season vegetables, if desired, after microwaving or add salt to water in casserole before adding vegetables. (Salt sprinkled on vegetables before microwaving causes shriveling.)

Frozen vegetables purchased in 6- to 10-ounce bag or box should be microwaved as directed on package.

INDEX

V.P., Publisher: Anne M. Zeman
Project Editor: Rebecca W. Atwater
Editorial Assistant: Rachel A. Simon
Photographer: Anthony Johnson
Food Stylist: Paul Grimes
Designers: Patricia Fabricant, Frederick J. Latasa
Production Manager: Lessley Davis
Production Editor: Kimberly Ebert